Anne Emily Garnier Newdigate-Newdegate

The Cheverels of Cheverel Manor

Being the Correspondence of Sir Roger and Lady Newdigate

Anne Emily Garnier Newdigate-Newdegate

The Cheverels of Cheverel Manor
Being the Correspondence of Sir Roger and Lady Newdigate

ISBN/EAN: 9783337112844

Printed in Europe, USA, Canada, Australia, Japan

Cover: Foto ©ninafisch / pixelio.de

More available books at **www.hansebooks.com**

THE CHEVERELS

OF CHEVEREL MANOR

BY

LADY NEWDIGATE-NEWDEGATE, ed.

AUTHOR OF 'GOSSIP FROM A MUNIMENT ROOM'

WITH ILLUSTRATIONS FROM FAMILY PORTRAITS

LONGMANS, GREEN, AND CO.
39 PATERNOSTER ROW, LONDON
NEW YORK AND BOMBAY
1898

CONTENTS

INTRODUCTION xi

CHAPTER I
1719-1776

Birth and parentage of Sir Roger Newdigate—King's Scholar at Westminster School—University College, Oxford—Founder of the Newdigate Prize—Member for Oxford—First marriage to Sophia Conyers—Second marriage to Hester Mundy—Letter from the latter to Sir Roger—Lady Newdigate's letters from Newnham 1

CHAPTER II
1781

Life at Buxton as described by Lady Newdigate—Letters from Charles Parker and Nelly Mundy—Visit to Manchester—Return to Buxton and home 13

CHAPTER III
1781

Lady Newdigate's second visit to Buxton *via* Shipley—Letters to Sir Roger—Visit to Sheffield—Lady N.'s illness—Her recovery 29

CHAPTER IV
1782-1785

Lord Bagot's announcement of the birth of a son—Lady N.'s letters from London on the eve of a general election—Death of Mrs. Ned Mundy—Lady N.'s visit to Buxton *via* Shipley—Lady N.'s letters from London, 1785—Charles Parker's embryo love-affair with Miss Howe—His marriage to Miss Anstruther 49

CHAPTER V

1787-1788

Lady Newdigate's letters about her brother's courtship of Lady Middleton from Shipley and Bath—Mr. Mundy's engagement and second marriage—First mention of Sally Shilton—Grand concert at Derby—Lady N.'s account of it and visit to Shipley 68

CHAPTER VI

1789

Lady Newdigate in London—Birth of Lady Middleton's daughter—Lady N. at the Birthday Drawing-room—Her return to Arbury—Recalled by illness and death of Lady Middleton—Her will—Large provision for the baby 81

CHAPTER VII

1790-1794

Lady Newdigate's sittings to Romney for her portrait—Lady Templetown's letters—Death of Motta at Arbury—Letter of Mrs. Newdigate, with account of day spent at Naples with Sir William and Emma Lady Hamilton 98

CHAPTER VIII

1792

Sally Shilton brought to London for her musical *début*—Her success at private parties—Her prospects of becoming a professional singer—Lady Newdigate at Court for the presentation of her niece Fanny Mundy, afterwards Lady Charles FitzRoy 109

CHAPTER IX

1792

Sally's continued success as a singer at drawing-room parties—Her breakdown in health—Abandonment of all idea of a professional career for Sally 122

CONTENTS

CHAPTER X
1792-1795

Sally goes to Lisbon for the winter—Her letter from thence to Sir Roger—Birth of a son to Charles Parker—Letter from Mr. Mundy describing the reception at the Opera of the news of Lord Howe's victory on the 1st June, 1794—Death of Charles Parker 137

CHAPTER XI
1795

Lady Newdigate's journey to Sussex with Mrs. Barton—Their stay at Stansted Park—Expedition to Portsmouth and the Isle of Wight—They leave Stansted for Bognor Rocks . . 150

CHAPTER XII
1795

Life at Bognor Rocks—Visit from the Duchess of Devonshire—Return to Stansted—Home by Harefield 164

CHAPTER XIII
1797

From Arbury to Piccadilly—Illness of Lord Charles FitzRoy—Lady Newdigate's arrival at Brighton—Life in lodgings—Sketches of Cliff and Steyne 175

CHAPTER. XIV
1797

Letters from Brighton (*continued*)—Arrival of Prince of Wales—Brighton Races—Lady Charles FitzRoy's illness—Lady N.'s change of lodgings—Death of Lady Charles FitzRoy at Wandon 192

CHAPTER XV
1797-1800

Lady Newdigate's visit to Margate—Her last letters to Sir Roger—Her failing health—Her death—Prayer found in her pocket—Her will 211

CHAPTER XVI

1797 1806

Sally Shilton's reputation as a singer—Her marriage—Mr. and Mrs. Ebdell's letters to Sir Roger—King George III. expected at Packington—Sir Roger's offer of Sally's musical services on the occasion—Lord Aylesford's answer—Sir Roger's declining health—His death 218

CONCLUSION 227

LIST OF ILLUSTRATIONS

SIR ROGER NEWDIGATE . . . . *Frontispiece*
From the portrait by Romney.

NELLY MUNDY . . . . . . *To face p.* 30
From the portrait by Sir Joshua Reynolds.

GEORGIANA, LADY MIDDLETON . . ., 68
From the portrait by Hoppner.

HESTER, LADY NEWDIGATE . . . ,, 98
From the portrait by Romney.

CHARLES PARKER AND JANE ANSTRUTHER ,, 142
From miniatures (said to be) by Cosway.

LADY CHARLES FITZROY . . . . ,, 210
From the portrait by Hoppner.

Lady Newdegate wishes to acknowledge with gratitude Mr. Mundy's kind permission to reproduce three of his family portraits at Shipley for this book. They are the following: 'Nelly Mundy' by Sir Joshua Reynolds, 'Lady Middleton' by Hoppner, and 'Lady Charles FitzRoy' by Hoppner.

INTRODUCTION

It must still be within the memory of the present generation when George Eliot first made her mark as a writer of fiction in the pages of 'Blackwood's Magazine.'

Her 'Scenes of Clerical Life' revealed to an admiring public the pathos, caustic humour, poetical fancy, and keen insight into character of a new and unknown writer. In this her first work of imagination George Eliot appears at her simplest and consequently at her best. Inspired by memories of her early youth, she wrote from her heart as well as from her head, and her characters with their life tragedies impress us the more because they are taken from real life and from amongst her personal surroundings. She speaks of these three stories herself as 'a bit of faithful work that will perhaps remain like a primrose in the hedgerow and gladden and chasten hearts in years to come.'

Nowhere did these charming tales excite keener interest than in a far-away corner of Warwickshire. The inhabitants of this particular neighbourhood were naturally somewhat exercised in their minds in regard to the identity of this unknown George Eliot. It was clear he must have had unusual opportunities of intimate acquaintance with places and people still in evidence to prove how graphically they had been portrayed. Squires, parsons, doctors, lawyers, &c., were depicted with a kindly yet satiric pen, apt to note down any peculiarity or weakness as well as more flattering characteristics. Friends and neighbours readily fitted the caps on to each other's heads, not altogether without a spice of malice in their amusement. Here and there personalities were so thinly veiled that it would have been impossible for those indicated to avoid recognising their own portraits, though occasionally with decided reluctance.

Have we not heard how 'Mr. Farquhar, the secondary squire of the parish,' characterised by a well-known lisp, made a feeble protest against this imputation in the following appeal to his medical friend and adviser:

'*You* know, Mithter N., that I never lithp exthept when my thtomach ith out of order.' So loth are we to acknowledge our slight infirmities.

Nevertheless the first editions of George Eliot's works were exceedingly popular in the neighbourhood, and soon written keys were passed round giving the real names of places and people side by side with the author's slightly disguised nomenclature.

It is rarely any writer can venture to utilise so boldly the localities and experience of actual life. When Mary Anne Evans (or Mrs. Lewes as she then called herself) began to write fiction she probably felt that by her own act she was finally separated from her family and the home of her youth. She had besides veiled her identity under an incognito so complete that not even her publishers knew her sex and her real name. Thus she felt free to dive into the recesses of a singularly observant and retentive mind, and make use of the stores of fact and fancy she had accumulated during her apparently quiet and uneventful girlhood.

We can understand how completely at home she would be amid the surroundings of farmhouse life, and how well acquainted she would naturally become with the petty gossip, local scandals, and severe but often just criticisms of a middle-class country neighbourhood. In the pictures she draws from life in this class not even her nearest relatives have escaped her humorous and graphic pen.

The 'Scenes of Clerical Life' comprise three stories. In the first and last George Eliot has not scrupled to take her plots from tragic circumstances still within the knowledge of the living.

In the second tale, 'Mr. Gilfil's Love-story,' the date of its occurrences carries us back to the eighteenth century, and there were no existing susceptibilities that could be wounded by her realism at the date of its publication. The scene of that pathetic story is laid at Arbury in Warwickshire—the Cheverel Manor of George Eliot—whilst Sir Christopher and Lady Cheverel are intended to represent Sir Roger Newdigate and his second wife.

It is at first sight surprising how this authoress can have acquired so much knowledge of the internal life of a family who lived long ago, and were dead many years before she was born. It has been accounted for in the following manner.

Robert Evans' first wife (not George Eliot's mother)

had been a valued member of the household at Arbury.[1] She must have had ample opportunity of hearing the usual gossip handed down by housekeeper to housekeeper concerning the doings and sayings of the family. In those days, when feudalistic veneration still flourished, these traditions were reckoned of greater importance than since the world has moved onward at a giddy pace, and levelling influences have been at work and are working for good as well as for evil. No doubt the stories from the big house were treasured up in the immediate neighbourhood, and by none more than by the estate bailiff's little daughter.

Mary Anne Evans was born at the South Farm, within the precincts of the park at Arbury, and she has told us herself how later on she used to be her father's constant companion in his business expeditions. Whilst Robert Evans was transacting estate work with the Squire in the library, she probably waited for him in the housekeeper's room at Arbury.

This picturesque old room has been accurately described by her and appears in more than one of her works. Here she must have heard much discourse on the past and present, of which she has given us amusing specimens, showing that the speakers, if truly reported, could have taken little account of the presence of so quiet and retiring an auditor. It was probably through the favour of the housekeeper that George Eliot obtained her knowledge of the rest of the house, whilst her descriptions of Sir Christopher and Lady Cheverel are evidently taken

---

[1] Her epitaph in Astley Church is as follows:
'In Memory of HARRIET, wife of ROB^T EVANS, for many years the Friend and Servant of the Family of Arbury.
Ob^t 26th Dec. 1809.
Æt 39.'

from the full-length portraits of their originals in the saloon at Arbury.

The story of the heroine of the tale—Caterina—being founded on fact, would be very likely to have impressed an imaginative and romantic girl, more especially as in her youth there would be many still alive who could remember the 'little syren' with the big dark eyes and the beautiful voice who came from the big house to be the mistress of the vicarage.

In the following pages we may be able to judge how far George Eliot was true to the life in the facts and characters of this one tale.

Amongst the numerous letters preserved in the muniment-room at Arbury there are many written by the Lady Cheverel who was Caterina's patroness. These letters, from which the following extracts have been made, have no pretensions to any special value as historical records. They are merely mementoes of the life of the period in town and country. They will be found full of domestic details, descriptive of the writer's various interests and pursuits. They also contain the relation of the loves, joys, and sorrows of a warm and affectionate heart given with all the frankness of intimate correspondence.

But the Cheverels of 'Mr. Gilfil's Love-story' shall be left to unfold their own characters and manner of life as far as possible from their letters written and received.

THE
CHEVERELS OF CHEVEREL MANOR

CHAPTER I

1719–1776

'Well, that theer's whut I coal a pictur',' said old 'Mester' Ford, a true Staffordshire patriarch, who leaned on a stick and held his head very much on one side, with the air of a man who had little hope of the present generation, but would, at all events, give it the benefit of his criticism.

'Th' yoong men noo-a-deys the'r poor squashy things—th' looke well anoof, but the' woon't wear, the' woon't wear. Theer's ne'er un 'll carry his 'ears like that Sir Cris'fer Chuvrell.'

. . . . . .

It was ten years at least since Sarti had seen anything so bright, stately, and beautiful as Lady Cheverel.—MR. GILFIL'S LOVE-STORY.

SIR ROGER NEWDIGATE was born May 20, 1719. He was the seventh son and youngest child of Sir Richard Newdigate, third baronet, by his second wife, Elizabeth, daughter of Sir Roger Twisden, Bart. Sir Richard died in 1727, and was succeeded by his eldest surviving son, Sir Edward, a boy of twelve, who died under age in 1734. At his death the only surviving and youngest brother, Roger, then a King's Scholar at Westminster School, succeeded as fifth baronet, but leaving no issue the baronetcy became extinct in 1806. Sir Roger's three sisters, who all predeceased him, married respectively the Honourable John Chichester,[1] Mr. Palmer,[2] and Mr. Ludford.[3]

[1] Mrs. Chichester's son succeeded his uncle as fifth Earl of Donegal in 1757.
[2] Charles Palmer, Esq., of Ladbroke, co. Warwick.
[3] John Ludford, Esq., of Ansley, co. Warwick.

B

Shortly after Sir Roger's death an appreciative notice of him appeared in the 'Gentleman's Magazine.' This was followed a few months later by a longer memoir in the same publication by the Rev. R. Churton. We here make a few short extracts from these papers.

'The incomparable baronet of Arbury,' as his biographer styles him, 'was a lover of *virtu* and an excellent classic from his early days, and made two lengthy tours on the Continent, where he accumulated many objects of art, which now adorn his Warwickshire home. . . . The best classics, and Homer in particular, seemed as familiar to him when he was on the other side of fourscore as if he was just come from Oxford or Westminster. . . .

'To the University of Oxford he was a steady friend and frequent benefactor, especially to University College, where he matriculated. . . . Amongst his testamentary bequests was the sum of 1,000*l.* on trust for an annual prize for English verses on ancient sculpture, painting, and architecture. The prize was brought forward in his life-time, when he expressed two conditions only, that there should be no compliments to himself ("if there is it will make me sick"), and that the number of the lines should not exceed fifty. When he was asked: "Will you not allow another fifty?" "No, no," he said, "I won't tire them in the theatre." Later on he observed on the same subject: "Our great fault is want of compression. The best of Horace's odes and the finest Psalms are seldom more than about that length."'

In this simple fashion the 'Newdigate' Prize for Poetry was founded at Oxford.

Sir Roger's connection with the University was of long duration and of a flattering nature. In 1749 he had the degree of LL.D. conferred upon him, and the following year he was first elected to represent Oxford in Parliament.[1] In accordance with the rules of the University he was unaware he had been proposed and elected until he received a letter from the Vice-Chancellor informing him of the honour conferred upon him.

'In the same manner, without application or expense whatsoever, he was re-elected five times . . . until in 1780, after thirty-five years' service in Parliament . . . he solicited his dismission and retired from public life.'

In politics Sir Roger was a rigid Tory of the old type, whilst Horace Walpole calls him 'a half-converted Jacobite.'

'In person,' says Archdeacon Churton, 'he was above the middle size, a true English gentleman of polished manners, and of the old school. There was about him a dignified affability of deportment, and at the first interview with a friend his fine open countenance was lighted up with a blended radiance of intelligence and benevolence, which those who saw it often cannot adequately describe, but no one who once saw it will ever forget. . . .'[2]

Sir Roger Newdigate married early, and shortly after his return from the foreign tour, which followed immediately on his leaving Oxford. The wife of his youth was Sophia, daughter of Edward Conyers of Copt Hall, Essex, and of the Honourable Matilda Fermor, daughter of Lord Lempster.

Arbury contains many relics of Sophia, Lady Newdigate, who seems to have been as artistically endowed as her husband. But as she was not the original of George Eliot's Lady Cheverel we need only record that after a long and happy married life of thirty-one years she died in 1774, leaving no children behind her.

[1] He had previously been elected as Knight of the Shire for Middlesex in 1742.
[2] *Gentleman's Magazine*, 1807.

Sir Roger was for a time inconsolable, and sought distraction in a prolonged tour on the Continent—the second he made during his life. Whilst sojourning in Italy this time he added largely to his collection of pictures, engravings, coins, books and statuary, which he had commenced in earlier days.

It was not until after his return to England that he first met the lady who was to become his second wife, and was destined to figure in the pages of 'Mr. Gilfil's Lovestory.'

Hester Margaretta Mundy was the daughter of Edward Mundy of Allestree in Derbyshire, and of his wife Hester, daughter and eventual heir of Nicholas Miller of Shipley in the same county. This lady, the object of Sir Roger's second choice, must have been a very attractive woman both in looks and disposition, though no longer in her first youth. Their marriage took place after a short courtship on June 3, 1776, at which period Hester must have been nearer forty than thirty years of age, though quite eighteen years younger than her husband.

During her twenty-four years of married life the second Lady Newdigate was a voluminous letter-writer. She had many opportunities for exercising her aptitude with her pen, owing to Sir Roger's disinclination to leave his Warwickshire home, which increased as years grew upon him, so that his wife had frequently to make her excursions without him. Hester was evidently an especial favourite with her own near relations, and was often called away to participate with them in seasons of sorrow and anxiety as well as of joy. In later life when ailing in health she was absent for weeks at a time in search of relief at English watering-places. On all these occasions her letters to her husband are almost journal-like in their fulness of detail—a minuteness and particularity he seems to have demanded and thoroughly appreciated.[1]

Sir Roger has preserved this correspondence carefully divided into separate packets, each of which represents an absence varying from a few days to a few weeks. Many of the letters have been docketed by him with the dates when they have been received, though Hester almost

---

[1] Sir Roger seems to have been fully as regular in his replies. Unfortunately his letters have not been kept.

always omitted the month and year when she wrote to him. In transcribing the following extracts all eccentricities and faults of spelling have been retained as they were written.

The earliest letter in Hester's handwriting is one written just after her engagement to Sir Roger had taken place, when she was still Miss Mundy. It begins, as nearly all hers do, without any formal address.

All Friday & yesterday I pleased myself with the Idea that by to-night's post I sh'd write you a very saucy Letter; two very tollerable nights rest had done more towards calming my spirits & easing my Heart than all your generosity, tender affection & every healing Balm you strove to administer could effect. I have really been a very rational creature, last night went through a most furious presentation at Lady Williams' & did not so far expose myself as to make your very good friend and mine, Miss Conyers [1] blush for me. I have gone about my business with composure & flatter myself I have remember'd every thing you have said to me tho' my endeavours have not in everything succeeded, but business shall have no part in this Letter, my friends think I have taken too large a dose of it to-day & to that they attribute my present aching Head, but the truth is I was last night unable to command my Anxious thoughts to Rest. The pleasing prospect before me one moment promised me a Life of happiness with ye most worthy, estimable & agreable Man in ye World (nay, was I not afraid you w^d from the short knowledge we have had of each other suspect my Sincerity) I w^d add the only Man upon Earth that I think could make me truely bless'd. Y^e next moment Rocks

---

[1] Miss Mary, or Molly, Conyers, the sister of Sir Roger's first wife.

appear'd which made me think, the greatest of which are my own unworthyness, and ye utter impossibility of my Ever obtaining any better hold of your affections, than what your blind partiallity now gives me & which I much fear will diminish as you become more clear sighted. Yet you shall never upbraid me with having deceived you. I confess that I do not, nor ever will deserve you, so you had better consider what you are about, & take a little more time to consider than you seem enclined to do.

I must thank you for a most flattering, soothing & pleasing Letter, but dare not attempt to answer it. Indeed my good Friend and Sister in Spring Gardens [1] with whom I dined charged me to write but Little and then go to Bed, in both which I obey her in hopes that a good Night will inspire me with so much pride and impertinence as I was possess'd of yesterday. Good night my dear Friend, accept the affectionate thanks of a most grateful Heart and which is wholelly

Y^{rs}
H. M.

Monday night.

A few months after Hester had become Lady Newdigate, Sir Roger seems to have been called away to London, probably on Parliamentary business, and their first parting took place. During her husband's absence, Hester went to stay at Newnham with her old friends Lord and Lady Denbigh. Here both she and her only unmarried sister, Nelly Mundy, appear to have been on terms of special intimacy with their host and hostess. Lady Newdigate sometimes speaks of Lady Denbigh as 'my mother,' which may mean her godmother, for her own parents had died some years previously.

---

[1] Sir Roger's town house.

Though Hester does not date her letters, we learn from her own words that these from Newnham were written within a year from the time she first met Sir Roger.

MY DEAR, DEAR RUNAWAY,—I could not begin a letter to you last night though inclination with a long train of powerful reasons pleaded for it. You see in this instance an exact picture of the state of my temper & the motive for my obstinacy will not soften ye colouring. The real truth is that I am a very bad dissembler & cannot appear what I am not, my spirits were foolishly low & I was afraid if you found it out your Vanity w^d lead you to suspect that your absence was ye cause. Indeed I could not myself find any *better* reason, for I was perfectly well, had a most kind and pleasant reception from my friend & sister, found the Latter in good health & the former recovering from a severe attack of her Billious Complaint & mending every hour, so that by the time we went to Supper everybody was jolly & happy excepting myself & I felt a weight at my Heart that would not let it rise but my *partie quarrée* with Susanah & the two elders has done wonders.[1] I now think of you no more & have been troting round my old Acquaintance in ye Shrubery with as much Glee as if I had not been transplanted into another Soil; but ye quantity of Rain that fell in ye Night has made ye walks so wett that I could not stay out as long as I wish'd to for my Companions are gone out on horse back & I had a momentary inclination to mount on a Pillion on the old Mare & make one of the Cavalcade, but you have so often express'd a fear of seeing me upon

[1] This probably refers to the warm baths Lady N. was in the habit of taking whenever an opportunity offered.

four legs that I felt a doubt whether you w^d approve. So ye old Lady was ordered into ye Stable & I am now much more agreably employ'd. We were so late before we left Coventry that I am afraid you would not get so far as you intended. We drank your health at 4 o'clock & at ½ past 9 when Lady D. wonder'd how you was at that instant employ'd, I boldly answer'd 'he is writing to me.' I shall often have that absurd fancy if you do not cure me of it.

Wednesday 2 o'clock.—In about 16 hours I hope to have the first Letter my Husband ever wrote me (for Lady D. sends to Rugby from whence they come early) & I just recollect this to be ye 1st time I ever address'd you in ye Character of a Wife & yet it seems so natural that I can hardly believe it. I find there is no need of practice on my Side to make ye pen run *glib* (do you understand that word?) therefore I entreat you give me no more opportunities of wearing out my fingers & your Patience in this way.

I have nothing of consequence to say but to remind you of your promise to be careful of yourself & to return to me as soon as possible. In that persuasion I shall be happy until the time arrives. Last year at this time I was so without knowing that you ever existed; see the mischief you have done me.

We read Gibbons (*sic*) last night & this morning has gone I don't know how. We were late at breakfast, then had prayers read by ye tedious Curate, after that a short walk which has brought us to ye end of the morning. . .

I have been thinking what you shall bring me from London Town and have determin'd it shall be a steal

Chain for my Watch. I will have nothing else for I shall not have a Want or Wish when I get you back again.

I have got 'Spieghero gli affetti mieci' from Mrs. Mundy; it is pretty and suits my present humour but not my abilities. I have try'd it but find it beyond me & is so in every sense, *& so & so* your dear Becky leaves you to imagine how much and how sincerely she is
Yours
HESTER NEWDIGATE.

Behold his Lordship just arrived. He travell'd late last night and was Rob'd a Little on this side Dunstable of 22 guineas & they took his Watch but on rec^t. of his purse return'd it. I hope you had no such Allarm. I will now go down and see the Peer.

Wednesday night 11 *o'clock.*—Tho' I am so sleepy I can hardly hold my eyes open I cannot go to bed till I have thanked my Dear Soul for a most sweet & kind Letter which I have just read over for ye third time & now I will pray for your preservation & happiness & then try if I can dream of you. Good night.

Friday.—So little sense had I last night that I mistook ye day of ye week (see ye date) and yet it was a Day I had look'd for with impatience & which brought me a most heartfelt pleasure. I hope to-morrow will do the same for I am foolish enough to wish to know what you do every hour. I would not for the world suspect that you are a bit wiser in regard to me, therefore I shall tell you that I slept well & that I and all my Companions have been in a perfect state of health all day.

My Lord routed us out ye moment we had breakfasted

to pass sentence upon some trees that are to be fell'd in the Garden. That done we continu'd our Walk and both ye day and our Party were so bright and agreable that not one of us recollected it was prayer day till near one o'Clock. Mr. Merrick had waited for us two hours & I fear will charge this unusual irregularity to my acc^t. Prayers over my three companions mounted their horses & I puzzled over 'Spieghero' but made nothing of it. The whole of this afternoon we have read Gibbons (sic) & are come to ye Chapters to which I believe he owes his fame; for I really think as a History it is a moderate performance. We have got Doct^r Watson's answer & intend to compare them as we go along. . . .

My Lord ask'd me this afternoon if I thought you would have any objection to his game keeper going over for a day to Arbury to beat for Wood Cocks with your keeper in your woods as they are birds of passage, here to-day & gone to-morrow. I thought there could be no objection & assented, but I have now taken fright not that I discover any cause, but I feel as if I had done wrong. If I have, reprove me as gently as you did *once* before, & I will love you the better for it. If you really do not disapprove I shall not be sorry to have a little emulation raised in our keeper by the puffing acc^t Mr. Ladbrook will give of his own performance. I do believe he is a very honest & excellent game keeper for I never saw a table so well supply'd. We have in ye 5 days that I have been here had 2 brace & ½ of partridges 7 Wood Cocks & 5 snipes.

I can't talk about Plays & Operas until we meet but am glad you are so Riotous. I read your News to Ld D. & he is happy with it & always wants more. Lady D. says no Latin lines shall draw me from Newnham till you leave London.

Y^e Dutchess of D. is charming. I hope you will bring a hair dresser down with you that can make me like her. Y^e story about Lady How is very pretty.

To-night I can use my warm Bath which I can if necessary repeat once or twice before I leave this place. I know it will take away my pains & releave my Spirits & your presence will perfect the cure. . . . . . . Nothing can be so fortunate for me as this opportunity of Bathing which I cannot at present do conveniently at home having neither Tub nor dressers.

Adieu,
Y^{rs} Ever.

Sunday evening.—This has been a sweet Cold Day for walking. I attended you in Idea from Church into the Park which I believe you only went through & made a doz. visits.

Lady Newdigate appear'd to-day for the first time at Kirby Church, very genteelly dress'd I thought, but she was greatly out done in height of Head and Ruffle by the young Ladies of ye Village. I trotted round ye Shrubery till I was quite Hot, which together with my Warm bath last night has made me quite alive & well. You can't imagine how much I find myself releaved by it. . . . . As to my Spirits they are rather above than below par. My Mother says I shall want backening if I bathe any more, which I shall certainly do & I believe on Tuesday because his Lordship goes from ye Mayor's Feast at Leicester to Ld Wentworth's for a night.

You will justly wonder what that can have to do with my Bath, but you must know it is prepared for me in ye Kitchen where he visits so perpetually that it is almost impossible to conceal it from him, & as he pretends to have heard & really seems fully persuaded that I am in a situation wch requires care, I know I sh'd be taken to task & have so many comments upon it that it would distress me. . . . I am sorry to disappoint him, but fear it is past doubt.

You begin your Letter like a dear Goose, & end it in the same stile. . . .

I wish you would get me some Sassiperella (I don't know whether I spell it right). I mean ye plant dry'd; it is given as an anti-scorbutic, whether sold at the Herb Shops or Apothecaries I know not, but if you want information confine your enquiries amongst ye Lower Class & don't say you want it for me, because there is a very ridiculous story annex'd to it which I will tell you if you don't know when you come down. It is late & I will be prudent. Adieu.

CHAPTER II

1781

Nature had given Captain Wybrow an admirable figure, the whitest of hands, the most delicate of nostrils, and a large amount of serene self-satisfaction; but as if to save such a delicate piece of work from any risk of being shattered she had guarded him from the liability to strong emotion. There was no list of youthful misdemeanours on record against him, and Sir Christopher and Lady Cheverel thought him the best of nephews, the most satisfactory of heirs, full of grateful deference to themselves, and above all things guided by a sense of duty.—MR. GILFIL'S LOVE-STORY.

TOWARDS the end of June 1781 Lady Newdigate paid a visit to Buxton in order to try a course of the waters, as a cure for the rheumatic pains and sleeplessness from which she had been suffering. She was accompanied by her sister, Nelly Mundy,[1] and by Sir Roger's cousin and supposed presumptive heir, Charles Parker, who at this date must have been in his twenty-seventh year. Sir Roger took the party to Buxton, established them there, and then returned to Arbury to look after his hay. He had retired from Parliament the previous year.

Lady Newdigate begins her journal-like correspondence immediately after his departure.

Saturday 8 o'Clock.—I can almost say with truth that I have at this instant no uneasiness but what your Absence occasions; it has not been so all day, but no doubt every occurrence & sensation has taken a colouring from it. Indeed we have all been foolish & Low, Charles and Nelly have scarcely utter'd a word except on y^c subject of your

[1] Nelly Mundy was two years Hester's junior, and the only unmarried member of the family. She seems to have been in great request, especially in times of sickness and trouble.

Journey, for which I felt oblig'd as it is the only one my heart can joyn in at present. To-morrow I hope to be wiser.

What a bold man you are to hazzard your wife's Character at such a Place as Buxton by sending a Lattin note open by a Postillion! I daresay it had been read by Doc^{tr} Robertson and all ye Learned Men here before it came to my hands. Well, I may be proud to be thought capable of inspiring such sentiments & not ashamed to understand & return ye like tho' I cannot find so readily a quotation that will do Justice to my heart. I did not make it out entirely to my satisfaction & as Nelly & Charles were both present & eagerly enquiring the Contents of my Note I was vain enough to show it to ye Latter & to make him explain it, which he did in very Elegant words. . . . We are as to numbers much as when you left us, but two-thirds at least are new and are like those they follow, equally unknowing and unknown. The Howes[1] are constant in their attention to us, indeed Lady H. is as anxious about me as if I was her sister. . . .

9 *o'Clock.*—We have pray'd, Jumbled & drank Tea, Charles is gone to sup above to see ye humours of ye Company whilst we finish our post. . . . I am pure well this evening & mean to try again to sleep without assistance.

Then follows a postscript from Nelly Mundy:

Here come I with my *mouse flies*, but the Dear Naughty Hetty has left me nothing to say . . . she tells me she

---

[1] Viscount Howe, the celebrated Admiral, who was advanced to an earldom in 1788. He married Mary, daughter of Chiverton Hartopp, Esq., of Welby, Notts.

has given a full acc^t of herself, if she has I'm sure it is a mighty pretty story. . . . I hope to be able to say at least as pleasant things next post so I will leave you to your Haymaking when I have made my Complaints of my flirt. Why did not you take him away with you? He has now told me in plain terms that I am so bold & ugly he can't bear to look at me. This is a breach you may believe that never can be made up. . . .

Y^{rs},
MOUSEY.

Lady Newdigate writes next:

Monday evening.—This has been a good day . . . have been more free from head than usual . . . & been very pretty company all day. I don't know whether Nelly & Charles will vouch for that but I daresay ye Viscount [Howe] will, with whom I have flirted many times to-day. They came & sat by us whilst we devour'd our Arbury pine though they would not partake, & we drank our Tea with them and ye conversation was kept up very pleasantly till Supper bell rang. Charles & his Lordship are sworn friends. I begin to suspect ye former worms himself into ye good graces of ye Latter by your order, to find out his sentiments in regard to me. Now I'll give the pen to Charles.

From Charles Parker on the same sheet:

I take it for granted Lady N. has sent you the fullest account of herself, therefore will not presume to say anything more. . . . Nelly is honest enough to confess that she has put some of my speeches in no favourable light. But worst of all! I have made a sad Blunder this

Evening to Lady Howe—which his Lordship did not let slip. I must seriously recollect myself & be more upon my Guard. I must now make my Complaints. They tell you I went to the Supper last night to see the Company, the fact was They would give me none, but told me, like little Eliza, that Tea was to be my Supper & so to Bed. After such usage you may guess we shall not be very cordial and I shall be ready to hatch up any Mischief agst them. I shall be a good Spy whose chief Excellence consists of being as Ill-natured as possible. We shall be at constant Variance, so come as soon as you can & keep us from any further Mischief. Adieu.

Lady Newdigate writes:

Tuesday.—I bathed before dinner thought ye Bath pleasant as I had it all to myself & found that ye Bath Maid could swim. I took her in to give me a Lesson. I believe I sh'd make something out of it if she could attend me constantly, but ye like favourable opportunity may not happen again whilst I stay.... We have had right Buxton weather ever since you went, ye way to ye well almost impassable. They laid planks over ye hollow for some days which danced as we went over & splashed us. Now they have fill'd it up with dirt and made it much worse. We have been forc'd to get high Pattins & with them we do vastly well. It is a fine afternoon but I doubt will rain again. I long to hear it is sunshine at Arbury, when will you bring it back to us? Y^r Hay wants it at present & indeed I am not so selfish to wish you with me just now, for you could not get out for Amusement or health.

From Nelly Mundy

'Tis very hard upon poor me, I really can't get in a word edgeways. Charles promised to leave me a page & did it in a delightful awkward puzzling manner: then comes this vile Hetty & fills it all up with all the news of the place & every thing worth relating except that *I am in great spirits*, wch is I know as important a piece of intelligence as you can receive. . . .

From Lady Newdigate

Thursday.— . . . A parcel of Vulgars arrived just at dinner time yesterday & took possession of our places & w^d not give them up which w^d have made an unpleasant Riot had not ye Howes taken us to their Table. . . . We had a famous Ball last night, 9 or 10 Couple with many Beauties from y White Hart, but Charles w^d not notice them. We did prevail on him to ask Miss Butterwick & Miss Dawson but they being engaged he w^d dance with nobody but Nelly. . . .

From Nelly Mundy

Buxton, July the 13*th.*—Lady Howe being gone out of Airing with Lady N. & Charles on horseback, I for once have an opportunity of getting the start of both in beginning a Letter to you, & thank God I have a very pleasant story to tell for our dear Hetty has had as much refreshing sleep as the various noises w^d admit of, & a repetition of those disturbances are prevented in future by the very friendly attention of L^d and L^{dy} Howe who insist upon exchanging apartments. Hetty objected strongly, upon wch it was refer'd to me & as I have no Idea that such a proposal cou'd Occur to any body who had not goodness of heart enough sincerely to wish it might be accepted, I at once acquiesced in the thing, but thought it incumbent on us to make it as little inconvenient to them as possible, therefore we call'd in Mrs. Fox [the landlady] & have with her assistance procured another dressing room for Ld Howe & prevented the necessity of their quitting their Bed Chamber & this has quieted all scruples of Conscience amongst us. . . .

We had a great many beauties here on Wednesday night & Charles Parker gave a fresh instance of his partiality for Old Women by slighting them all to dance with me. . . . I need not tell you I hope that I will take all possible care of our Dear Invaluable Treasure, or that we all love you and that I am,

Most affectionately y^rs
N. Mundy.

From Lady Newdigate

Saturday, 2 o'clock.—If I was not afraid of your very jealous disposition I sh'd be tempted to own that the last 2 days & nights have entirely reconciled me to ye Loss of you. You have no Idea how ye Noise, confusion & various *agrémens* of this place are increased. We are now fuller than any of my Bee hives for we send out swarms every night to ye neighbouring Lodging houses & take them into feed in ye day, a practice they say unknown before.

Nelly told you yesterday how very friendly L^d and Lady Howe had been in offering to change appartments with us. I sh'd have been quite unhappy to have accepted so much as that, & yet I really think if I could not have got a quiet Room by any other means I must have done so or have removed to some other house, but very fortunately we have accommodated matters so well that I have every advantage from their attention without any inconvenience to them, except Ld Howe's being without a dressing Room for one day. I wish'd to have waited till he got one, but he very Politely & kindly made his Serv^{ts} remove all his things into their Bed Chamber & insisted on my sleeping in the Lamb, for so my habitation is call'd & well deserves ye Name, for I heard nothing. . . . To give you an Idea of our Numbers I need only tell you that ye instant I left my Room Lady Gallway, her Sister & two Maids went into it. There they all sleep, dress, etc. In short it's ye only Room they have to retire to. The Edmonstones have the Parlour Mrs. Ratliffe quited. They are magnificent People indeed, have a most splendid Equipage with supporters & four fine horses, 2 Laced postillions, serv^t out of livery, footmen I know not how many, etc. In short neither the Howes nor Lady Newdigate are worthy regard before them. He is a Nova Scotia Baronet & fancys he is to take place of all English Bar^{ts} but they tell me we are not to let him. If that is really so & they give themselves airs I shall be apt to walk before her Ladyship in a quiet way when occasion offers. Both he and She seem mighty distant, but perhaps we may mistake ye Motive.

Ten at Night.— . . . We have a scheme of getting for a couple of Nights out of this Buxton Fog, Noise & confusion which nothing but ye efficacy of these Waters could enable one to live a week in. I sh'd be happier if I knew you approved our Plan but flatter myself you will. We mean to set out as soon as prayers are over in our Chaise, send Mrs. Lowe before to walk up y" Hill, then take her in & proceed gently to Dishly, Dine & stay there 2 or 3 hours & then proceed to our friend Starkie at Manchester with whom we shall spend a quiet day & return in the same gentle manner on tuesday which I think will do us good & our horses no harm.

Nelly Mundy writes :

Dishly 5 o'Clock.—We arrived here at 3 are just going to proceed to Manchester, have had a charming pleasant morning airing expect the evening to be as refreshing & beneficial after a most Luxurious Dinner of Mutton Steaks, Rost Chicken, Pease & tart eaten with a good appetite. . . . You can't imagine how we have enjoy'd our quiet dinner in a neat pretty room looking into beds of flowers & flowering shrubs . . . the Chaise is order'd so adieu.

From the same

Manchester Monday morning.—When we arrived here we were told that the South post did not go out till Eleven this morning, so I kept the Letter to give you the latest account. She bore her journey vastly well tho' the last 14 miles were very Stoney & made her head ache a little but a dish of Tea refresh'd her. . . . . It is a lovely day. This will be a Charming Hay Day for you. I hope we shall all do our Work well, God Almighty prosper us !

Y^{rs} etc.,

N. M.

From Lady Newdigate

Starkie Castle Monday.—Not a word of thanks did I send in ye Letter that went this Morn for a pretty piece of folly which came enclosed in yours. Indeed my dear Life you are too good to me, it is an odd thing to say but very true that ye flattery you bestow upon me makes me feel more humble than anything I ever met with, because I am conscious that I owe it more to your partiallity than to your Judgment, but don't you examine that point too nicely. It is proper that I sh'd be sensible of it & that I sh'd endeavour to be the being you so fondly paint. I will indeed my dear Love, my heart feels as it ought every instance of your kindness & does not yield to yours in warmth of affection, tho' I have not a pen that can speak it so agreably. God bless you, write on & never grow wiser.

Starkie is ye happiest of all mortals, she Lodges us very Comfortably; her house is quite a Little Baby House, delightfully situated for a town, Looking into Gardens & so quiet after ye Noise of Buxton, that it will require some resolution to return. . . . If I am stout to-morrow will go in my Chaise to the Infirmary to see these curious Baths the fame of which make a topic of conversation at Buxton. They say they are superior to any in this or any other Kingdom.

Starkie desires to add her Comp^{ts}.

From the same, from Buxton

Friday 11 o'C.—Lord Howe is just going to send a Servt to Middleton who will put this into ye Post to-night at Lichfield. Y^e Death of Mr. Whetham is y^e

cause of this messenger being sent. Lady Howe supposes the two sisters to be at Middleton & means to go to them if they wish for her;[1] she will be a real Loss to me but indeed I meet with many friends. Sneyd girls are come, both pretty but Mary quite Beautiful. Adieu. Venison was delightful & ye Bones pick'd.

Lady Newdigate's next letter begins with a graphic account of how she doctored herself for a headache with an emetic followed by six opium pills, with lamentable results, though after a bad day she was able to eat two wings of a boiled chicken at night. She goes on to say:

Poor dear Charles was so shocked when I came down last night & thought me so unable to sit up that he set off immediately in search of an Easy Chair or Couch, heard there was one at ye Grove Coffee House in a private parlour belonging to a Mr. & Mrs. Robertson. Away went he without knowing anything of ye people & beg'd they w^d give it up to me, which they very politely consented to & Just when I was thinking of returning to my Bed Chamber a most delightful Easy Couch made its entrance in at my Window, for it was too Large to gain admittance through ye Door. It is not to be imagined what instant relief it was to me. . . . I feel uncommonly well to-day, have been this Evening to wait upon Mrs. Robertson with my thanks and find she knows you . . . . and almost all my Connections. I met Mr. R. as I came out, he said a thousand Civil things about ye Dear Couch, desires me to keep it & wishes to see you. So do others

---

[1] In a later chapter we hear a great deal more of these two sisters, Mrs. Whetham and Lady Middleton, the daughters of Evelyn Chadwick, Esq., of Lincoln and West Leake, Notts.

also, yet I do not advise you to come yet, We are fuller
than ever, 69 were fed to-day at yᵉ Long Table & three
side Tables. Your Brother Baronet has made an attempt
to change yᵉ Dinner & Supper hours to 3 & 9 but it
does not take; they are very troublesome discontented
people. I believe if you had seen yᵉ beautiful Mrs. Fox
in Tears as I did last night you wᵈ have Challeng'd yᵉ old
Square Toes & poor Charles was in part yᵉ innocent
cause. It is quite impossible for him to keep out of a
Scrape. Being examined by yᵉ Bart in regard to our
Suppers and what we paid, he own'd that we were charged
but one Shilling & it seems they pay two. Upon this
Poor Mrs. Fox was attack'd & abused in very gross
terms. So in she came to us with streaming eyes to beg
we wᵈ explain to yᵉ Edmonstones that our Suppers were
never anything more than a Tart & Cold Chicken which
we Eat when yᵉ Company went to Supper above, whereas
the E....s order a hot supper of 5 or 6 dishes to be got at
9 o'Clock. I assured her I wᵈ do all in my power to set
yᵉ affair in its proper light which I have done, but her
Ladyship made me a Short answer & looks so haughty
& disagreable that I believe our Acquaintance will end
there. . . . What nice Venison you have sent this week!
yᵉ fattest that I ever tasted. Yᵉ Howes have also weekly
of which we partake & of most delightful Cherries,
Strawberries & Gooseberries fresh every other day from
Chadsworth. Yᵉ Pine, Melon & Apricots you sent were
also good, but it is quite grievous to see yᵉ total destruc-
tion of so much fine Orange & Myrtle. It is squeezed
irrecoverably & imbibed yᵉ smell of yᵉ Venison so
strongly that no Soaking in Water, Airing or other

means yet discovered will bring it about. Don't mangle ye poor Trees any more for us . . . ten O'Clock, my bathing hour so Adieu.

Sunday is properly a Festival & you have taken care I shall keep it as such. What a delightful Breakfast you sent me! Three packets containing 4 Letters, that is y^r product. . . .

At five yesterday Nelly & I went on ye Ashbourn Road attended by Lumber [a horse] with pillion & Charles's John to attend. At ye Carriers Inn I mounted & took ye opposite charming flat and striped Road between ye two Walls to the Village you & I first found out. It suits me so well that you may venture to suppose me trotting there every evening from six to seven. . . . At 10 went into ye Bath with Lettice my Mistress & ye two Nellys[1] as spectators. No ground can I gain or more properly I cannot lose it; in vain do I try to throw myself in as she does & skim along, down plump I go to ye Bottom. Nelly was much entertained with my very awkward attempts. . . .

Morning prayers were at ½ past 12 to-day & Evening at six, but I had half an hour's trot on ye Little Common by Fairfield. On our return coming over ye bridge a Post Coach & four drove full Gallop against us & had not the Gentlemen obliged ye Postillions to Stop w^d have canted us down the high bank into ye brook. They did Lock our Wheel but as Willm stood firm & they were stop'd in time we came off with a fright only. . . . Your restlessness about our continuance in this Noise has been of infinite advantage to us. I mention'd to ye Howes when at dinner

[1] Nelly Mundy and her maid, also called 'Nelly.'

to-day in more than usual Noise & heat that you wish'd me to Dine in my own Parlour, upon which Lady H. say'd why sh'd we not make a proposal of ye kind to Mrs. Fox. Accordingly it was done, agreed to, & we are the happiest people you can conceive with ye Idea of our quiet meals which are to begin to-morrow. God bless you, continue your good nights & when he thinks fit grant me ye like.

Tuesday.—Bath last night Charming, but make no progress in Swimming. Lettice says 'I am afraid y^r Lad^{sp} will never be bold enough,' but who knows what a fortnight more at Buxton may make of me. . . .

Charles Parker writes on the same sheet:

. . . How much longer are we to live with^t you? What can we do to entice you to us? Will a Mountebank, a Conjuror, a Raffle have any influence over you? Hoc juvat? I'm afraid you will go on to say: 'Horum semper ego,' etc. etc. What do you say to 60 People in the Long Room at an Assembly? (For these are the Joys of our dancing Days.) Will that do any better? 'No,' you will answer, 'still worse.' Well, now for my third and last expedient, I hope that will not fail to bring you. 'Tis the better Health & better Spirits of your dear Hetty, I hope in God we can promise you that, so Venez, voyez & Jouissez. Adieu. Good night.

CHAS. PARKER.

Nelly Mundy writes on Thursday night:

The Dear Soul has eat a good Supper of Plumb Pye & a glass of wine & is going in Glee to Swim. . . .

Never was so riotous a day as yesterday, Cottillions morning, noon & night, & after that singing & drinking Champagne till 4 o'Clock in the morning. Some of the men in bed all day to-day but enough *sober'd* to make out a Cottillion to-night. I believe I need not tell you that Charles took no Share of the Gallons of Wine that were swallow'd. I am apt to believe that he never does anything more wrong than making rude speeches to me. As I am left alone & have nothing more very interesting to tell you I'll go and see what the rioters are about, so good-night.

From Lady Newdigate

Friday, 5 o'C.—Bathing goes on (I had like to have said) swimmingly but that is not true. Lettice was mistaken in thinking I sh'd never be Bold. I can throw myself with a Spring forward upon ye Water & go plump to ye Bottom as direct as any stone, then shake my ears & try again with ye like success . . . but it is a charming exercise. Just as we were sitting down to dinner in Ld Howe's Parlour arrived my Brother;[1] he rode from Shipley & according to his usual Luck was twice wet to the skin. . . . They ask me if you will be here before Monday. I answer I know not when you come & I suppose you say it is my fault that you are not here now. Indeed, indeed my Dr Soul you w^d not be so happy with us as you are in y^r Hayfield for which I say don't come to make a Stay, only Just to take me out of Pawn.

---

[1] Edward Miller Mundy, Esq., of Shipley, near Derby, Lady Newdigate' only surviving brother and the youngest of the family. He was born in 1750.

There is one more letter from Lady Newdigate to her husband before he arrives to escort her back. In it she answers all his suggestions for their journey categorically, under numbered heads, and at the end goes on :

6^{thly} I do command you to come to Buxton as soon as possible after the rec^t of this Letter; Saturday I think sh^d be the Latest; 7^{thly} I rejoyce with you most sincerely that tuesday sennight is so near at hand & you will rejoyce still more with me that our pains & mortifications are likely to be well repaid. Indeed, indeed I am full of pleasing hope. . . .

In this batch of letters is included a paper in Charles Parker's handwriting, which contains some lines evidently composed by him, but largely corrected by Sir Roger's pen.

TO THE NAIAD OF BUXTON WELL

   Sweet Nymph that sporting in the tepid stream
   Shakest from thy auburn locks the roseate bloom
   Of Health & Joy, Haste thee sweet Nymph & shed
   Thy choicest influence o'er my Etta's Head!
       Haste thee sweet Nymph!
       And in its steamy Tides
       Whatever thy potent wave
       Under its limpid Crystall hides
   Present to close the languid aking eye
   And lull to sweet repose the lingering Sense.
       Haste thee sweet Nymph & shed
       On her thy choicest influence!

   Nor shall thou deem thy labor vain
   For ne'er did a more gentle Mind
   With manly sense & polish'd arts refin'd

Her well turn'd limbs plunge in thy mystic stream.
Haste thee Nymph & far away
Drive thrilling pain and wan inquietude
That tinges sickly pale the faded cheek
And writhing Spasm and wakeful lassitude
And whatsoe'er of ill yet lurks unseen
And whatsoever our trembling thoughts forebode
    Give to the saffron-robed Wye
To bear far off upon her rock-born Wave
In headlong plunges down her high wall'd course
To sanguine Derwent or Trent's stately Flood.
    Daughter of Phœbus and Hygeia fair
    Haste thee Nymph and hither bear
    Whate'er of healing drug or vapor bland
    Treasur'd in lofty caverns deep
    Midst thy fermenting minerals sleep,
    Potent the labouring limbs to free
    And sooth the pangs of misery.
Nor torture him who pendent o'er her couch
Now pours incessant vows before high heaven
    Now when she droops forlorn
    In sullen silence hides the wat'ry eye,
    Forbids the throbbing heart to move
    And checks the rising sigh.
    Haste thee sweet Nymph
    Two faithful hearts in one to save.
    So shall thy far fam'd Wave
Thro' distant lands in ages yet to come
    Be celebrated in poetic lore
Thy lovely flowing locks to bind
Grateful shall each the Chaplet weave
The laurell with the mistle intertwine
And Bladud's boasted springs shall yield to thine.

CHAPTER III

1781

Lady Cheverel . . . being herself on principle and by habitual self-command the most deferential of wives, she noticed with disapproval Miss Assher's occasional air of authority towards Captain Wybrow. A proud woman who has learnt to submit carries all her pride to the reinforcement of her submission and looks down with some superiority on all feminine assumption as 'unbecoming.'—MR. GILFIL'S LOVE-STORY.

IN the autumn of the same year, 1781, Lady Newdigate paid a second visit to Buxton for a supplementary course of the waters. She left Arbury on September 24 in company with her brother, 'Ned' Mundy. They got as far as his house, Shipley Hall, near Derby, the same evening, where they were welcomed by Fanny [Mrs. Mundy [1]] and Nelly, their unmarried sister.

Lady Newdigate writes to Sir Roger :

We got here by the Light of a Little clear Moon at little after seven, sh'd have had no need of its assistance had not ye nut of the fore wheel come off. Ned discover'd ye loss before the wheel follow'd it, so ye whole ended in a little delay & I have taken care to have it well secured against to-morrow. Fanny & Nelly were overjoy'd to see us, ye former looks better than I expected & seem'd in good spirits but Nelly whisper'd me that she was much

---

[1] Mrs. Edward Mundy was the daughter and co-heir of Godfrey Meynell, of Yeldersley, near Derby. She was in failing health at this time, and a visit to Lisbon had been projected for her benefit.

hurt & fretted with ye Contents of a Letter she found here from Mrs. Meynell disapproving entirely the Lisbon scheme, magnifying all ye difficulties & dangers of ye Voyage & telling her that her Uncle Doct^r Hunter of York is of opinion that ye sea sickness might be attended with ye most fatal consequences to her. Fanny soon after inform'd Ned of this & gave him ye Letter which he pocketed & beg'd the subject might not be enter'd upon till to-day. I see he is horridly vext but he utters nothing that can hurt her. They have had a long tête-a-tête since which she seems in better spirits, & has several times mention'd Lisbon as ye only place thought on, but I fear they will have a sad & perplexing scene to go through with ye Meynells to-morrow. Fanny seems very sorry that we don't stay to talk it over with them & has said all she can to persuade, but I plead your orders being peremptory & both Nelly & I are much obliged to you for giving us such a plea, for I am convinced if we were to give an opinion it w^d rather do harm than good. . . . Both Father & Mother seem inclined to committ Frederick & Henry to our Care ; they are two sweet Poppets, but quite of the fairy kind. . . .

What a Storm of Cold Wind have we had all last night and to-day ! to be sure it makes one Shudder with ye Idea of mounting ye Peak Hills but our object is profit & not pleasure so we shall not be discouraged. The dear Nelly seems quite happy that she has it in her power to devote herself to our Service. We mean to set out at 9 & hope to be at Buxton by ½ past 6 at y^e latest. . . .

Buxton, Wednesday night 9 *o'Clock.*—We arrived well & without any accident soon after seven. . . . Y^e Road

Mrs. Nelly Mundy

hinder'd us for y^e Lime Carts have cut it sadly, so we did not get to Matlock till ½ past one. I think I need not add that we were pretty well & Jolly when I have told you that on hearing the Company in ye Long Room were to dine in half an hour We preferr'd Joyning them rather than wait to have a dinner dress'd; but what was my astonishment to see no less than sixty covers laid & every place fill'd. We modestly took our Seats at ye Lower End which fortunately was one of ye warmest places in ye Room & ate up almost a whole Shoulder of Mutton & dish of Potatoes which stood by us, believing ourselves to be totally unknowing and unknown; but when hunger was satisfy'd & we began to look about us we discover'd at another table Lady Eliz. Chaplin, her three daughters, Lady Bromley, Miss Curzon (Ld Scarsdale's daughter), Mrs. Bathurst & old Hewitt of Nottinghamshire. As Lady E. Chaplin was a very Old Acquaintance we thought it right to make ourselves known, were very politely & kindly rec^d & much pressed to continue in their *Xmas party* for such they look upon it; the wind cannot be colder at that season.

On our arrival here we were shewn into our own parlour where there was a comfortable fire, so took it for granted all things were ready for our reception, but Mrs. Fox soon appear'd & discover'd to us that we were not expected till friday; my second Letter which told of our coming to-day is not arrived. So ye Rooms Mrs. Fox intended for us are wanted & the Lyon and Lamb engaged by the Ld President of Scotland till ye 1st Monday in Oct^{br} which is about the time she says we order'd them to be kept. But we have got a good well-aired double-bedded Room for to-night & I dare say shall be able to fix ourselves to our Minds to-morrow. . . . Good night, I am going to Bathe but not in my Cork Waistcoat as I find Mrs. Beresford bathes at ye same time.

Thursday morning 27th September.— . . . If I sh'd go to Sheffield which must depend on the Weather and my own Feelings, it will probably be about Monday sennight. You have given me Leave to have desert knives which it w^d be a pity not to have to suit ye others. My Brother has Knives & forks also made to suit his Silver ones, so exact that they can't be distinguish'd, which are used only in ye manner I proposed viz. : when ye others run short. The Carving Knives are also very handsome. I remember you liked them for that purpose at Wotton & Keel. Consider ye matter and Let me know your pleasure for I sh'd be sorry to go a Step beyond it. I have been interrupted by a Visit from Mrs. and Miss Anson. The former observed how comfortable we were in this Parlour, said she hoped we meant to Joyn them at dinner. I told her ye Weather was too severe for me an Invalid to hazzard being placed wth my Back to ye Door which I apprehended must be ye case if I went into ye Room above. She said yes that I certainly sh^d for they had been a Week in those cold places & were not much better off yet. She envied us our warm parlour & I am sure I sincerely pity them with twenty thousand a year & two Parlours disengaged ever since they came, that they chuse to submit to such hazzard and inconvenience.

I like my new Maid much, she is gentle & modest & seems as if she w^d be tidy. You will not think her

handsome enough, but she is not ugly & is very
genteel. . . .

We have got a Room which I think I shall like better
than ye Lyon. It is directly under it, is much more
cheerful & pleasant & I think must be as warm and
quiet, & ye next Room to it will be at Liberty to-morrow
so you may suppose us fairly settled.

I enclose Mr. Barton's[1] account for Tea, ye sum frights
one but if ye Common Tea runs (as Mr. B. says it does)
near 80p^{ds} ye Chest it will answer well. Y^e best is full 16^s
a pound but Mundys & Newdigates[2] who have also a
lot & who have also had from ye Shops since ye new
Tax was laid, say it is better than what you can buy for
18^s. I tell you all this to console you & further will
promise it shall last a great while. . . . I have used you
with uncommon ceremony, which I hope won't be lost
upon you, nothing but Gilt Paper could be got at Last
Night, but don't expect ye Like again.

Friday 2 o'Clock, Septr 28th.—Our plan of Living is
now so fixt that you may know where to find us any hour
of the day. We rise at 7, drink water till nine, Breakfast,
pray at 10, Jumble and trot from Eleven till one, drink
water, put on a clean shirt, dine at ½ past 2, write, read
work & play upon ye Guittar all ye Evening, sup at 8,
Bathe at 10 & then to bed. The Lyon & Lamb are
fools to our present appartment. I did not know there
were any so thoroughly comfortable & pleasant. L^d
President may stay as long as he pleases, I will not change

[1] James Barton, Esq., who was the husband of Lady Newdigate's youngest sister, 'Milly.'
[2] Francis Newdigate, Esq., of Kirk Hallam, Derbyshire, and his wife, *née* Sneyd.

... Don't be vext when you hear we did not get our things from Arbury yesterday. Y^e Carrier says his Waggon was so full he could not bring them, but that they positively will be here to-morrow morning. It is of no consequence, for Ned insisted on my Bringing a Bottle of his fine old Madeira for fear we sh'd not get good wine at Matlock & I have enough of it to last a day or two.

Do you know that we drink of ye old St. Ann? and that it is actually (notwithstanding all that Carr told you) more than a degree and half warmer than ye new Well. It seems that very soon after we went away ye Company wrote to Carr & insisted on having ye Old Well restored, or they w^d all leave ye place. He pleaded impossibility, the Wall of the Hotel, that is to be, being exactly built upon it, upon which some familys quited ye place & a parcel of spirited Men got some Masons & actually pick'd a Hole in ye Wall till they came to ye Spring. This brought an order from Carr (who durst not appear himself) to Arch over ye Spring, which is done in form of a little Nich just to prevent ye Rain getting in, & ye Old Women dip their glasses through a hole in ye Wall. That fine Octagon Building & fine Pump are entirely deserted, ye News of which was no sooner spread abroad than Company came in numbers from every quarter & continue to do so. God knows who they are but no less than seven post Chaises, a Post Coach & 3 Phaetons have arrived since yesterday morning. . . . Only think what the Old St. Ann may do for me when her deputy did so much! I expect to be so beautify'd & improved that you will not know me. . . . A thousand longings I have, one is for a Barrow of Griff[1] Coals, for these are detestable but cheap enough, sixpence a day for each fire be they great or small. . . .

Saturday Sepr 29th.—Another lovely looking day, but high cold wind. . . . Edwd goes behind ye Chaise & generally walks up the Hills, or I think he c^d hardly stand ye Cold, but I hear no complaints but of Lodging. They were ye 1st night in a Room with about a doz^n, where ye Wind blew through their Beds; they are now got into one which contains but 3 Beds but no warmer than ye first. I shall send for Mrs. Fox & make a rout but fear we shall get no redress. I believe I must offer to pay something for a room for them if I can't get one without. All ye footmen have got such Colds & Coughs that it is terrible to hear them as they stand at ye Door.

Sunday Sepr 30th.—It has poured all this Day with^{out} a moment's interruption or even Abatement, but with ye help of Pattins & Parapluies we got to ye Well. Old St Ann is rather nearer than ye New; the poor Dippers sit soaking without the least Shed to Cover them. It is cruel that they don't make them some shelter. . . . I fancy out of seventy-four that ye Long Room Contain'd to-day there might be six names (our two included) that are not unknown to you. Such a parcel of Shabs I never beheld. How did I rejoyce that you were not here. You c^d not play Whist all day with Mr. Anson & the Dundass's nor amuse yourself with Mr. W—kf—d's doleful face & conversation & there is nothing Else for you. I daresay we are abused for shutting ourselves up but it is impossible to go amongst them. . . . What a sad story

---

[1] The coal mine on the Arbury estate.

of yᵉ Poor Man kill'd in yᵉ Pits! too sick to dwell upon! We must turn our attention towards yᵉ Poor Widow & Children. . . . Yᵉ Carrier was honest, the things came yesterday & we tuned Guittars & strum'd most of the Evening but that circumstance made us acquainted with a most Cruel Loss. John Music is gone, yᵉ Dear Man that used to save me the trouble of tuning. We are going to Supper upon Craw Fish & Roasted Potatoes. . . . A Scrap from Shipley says that Lisbon will still be yᵉ Place.

From Nelly Mundy

Buxton, Monday.—The Date is very right, it has been a true Buxton Monday for it has rain'd the whole day. . . . We do not lose a single glass of water if it rains dogs and cats, the Pattins great Coat & large Umbrella are sufficient security. The upstairs party seems to be in a very fluctuating state, five or six carriages are gone off to-day & several arrived. . . . Lᵈ Vernon & the Bishop of Peterborough are expected on Wednesday. It is very immaterial to us who comes or who goes for we never mix with the Company but at prayers. . . . The most important events of this day I think are that Thoˢ has had a tooth drawn & that the Wheels of a Cart separated themselves from the Carriage as it was going up the hill, came down again by themselves & crack'd the Chaise that was waiting at the door. Fortunately for us it was not yours. . . .

Lady Newdigate goes on upon the same sheet:

Tuesday.—Another Rainy Day and dark as possible, but it brought *me* (Hester for fear you sh'd not know my hand) a sweet Letter so I defy the day to give me its colour. Bath^g at noon agrees well, & I swim like a frog that has lost ye use of its hind Legs. Don't go & maim a poor frog to see how that is. I assure you it is very tollerable. . . . I have had a Letter from Ned to-day so like himself that I w^d enclose it was it not for double Postage. He says he has stood firm in regard to ye Lisbon plan & has carry'd his point with less difficulty than he expected & that he hopes to begin to move ye 10th. They mean to go ye cross Country Road to Bath, so to Falmouth where a packet is order'd to be ready for them. So much was said of the badness of the Portugese ships that I suppose that plan was given up. I have desir'd Ned to send two Cribs that the Children sleep in to be at Arbury before they arrive there. . . . Poor Fanny's mind is torn to pieces so much about herself & Children that it makes dragons of Everything; one which perhaps you will think absurd, but which I could wish to humour her in for a short time if you will give me Leave. She recollects ye Cracks & sinking of ye Sealings in ye old Dining Room & Gallery & is unhappy about her Children sleeping in that part of ye house. Ned mentioned it to me at ye same time expressing entire confidence in your Judgment & tender care in not placing his babes where you was doubtful of their safety, but seem'd much to wish that Fanny might go away without that weight upon her mind. In consequence of the conversation I took an opportunity of saying to Fanny that I meant to place her babes for the Winter in ye Blue Room as it was so near that I c^d call in at all hours. I perceived her Countinance brighten immediately, so if you have no objection let it be so. If they are Noisy & disturb us we can move them afterwards. . . .

Wednesday Octr 3rd.—A most heavenly day. . . . We are now going to finish the evening as usual with Book, Work & Music; don't you want to know our Studies? We have just finish'd ye Sorrows of Werter, a novel which was much in Vogue last year. It is interesting but I think ye sentiments of the Hero often exceptionable. Y^e Author seems sensible of it & makes a sort of lame apology in the preface. We are now in Burney's travels through Germany, wch I once began & I believe was forc'd to return ye book.

Ld Vernon & ye Bishop of Peterborough are just arrived. We have sent Comp^{ts} & enquiries and ye Latter politely intends himself y^r *honor* of calling upon us to-morrow. He will be an acquisition to us. Y^e other is shy & says Little, perhaps may call at our parlour door once out of Civility but ye Lawn Sleeves will I hope like to visit us often. . . .

Thursday.—I believe I shall ruin you in tea & muffins, have just invited Ld Vernon, Ansons & Bishop of Peterborough for this afternoon & if I feel pretty well we will attend them for an hour into ye Card Room for I find People think we are Sulky & proud, that we keep so close in our hole. I deny that charge but believe ye truth is we are a Little nice & think time too precious a commodity to squander away in civilities to people that we neither expect or wish to see again. I don't like to be abused neither, so will try to stear between ye two extremes. . . . Last Night finish'd my 1st week. I paid my Bills £13. 14.—too much, but I don't know how to lessen expense, without lessening Comforts. That last word properly introduces ye subject of Sheffield goods, for I cannot help ranking in that class everything that tends to make ample provision of the useful in a family as it naturally introduces neatness order & convenience. I absolutely deny that your objections to y^e *shams* which you say my heart is so much set upon proceed either from Pride or Covetousness. If I thought the former sh'd wish some friend (for I durst not in that case do it myself) to put into your hand ye very instructive pretty fable of the Peacock & Golden Dish; but it is not applicable to your case. Do not either fear or flatter yourself that your passion for ye sort of intrinsic Worth now in question has anything to do with ye qualities of ye Mind. Our little differences in opinion are mear preventions form'd perhaps by Education & might in both have taken too strong a Colouring if each had been connected with a person exactly of their own way of thinking, ergo, it is better that we sh'd not always be of the same mind. But after all this learned Discourse I am still irresolute about going to Sheffield. On first reading your Letter I determin'd not to go; after a 2nd [reading] was afraid you w^d think I was Capcious, that you w^d not enter into all my follies. Now I think I see it in another light & that ye permission you give me to please myself is a proof that you have no objection but the *throwing* away (as you think) so much Money. Now in ye first place ye Money you gave me is for no other purpose than to fool away as I like, and in ye second it is fit that every one sh'd pay for their own Whims. You must & still more dearly for yours whenever your

Magnificence chuses to replace them with really Silver. I shall therefore go & give full scope to my extravagance looking upon it as a pretty & proper compliment to make myself a handsome present & rather a debt as I never have yet laid out any considerable sum for my own Gratification except on ye Monument to the memory of my D^r father & Mother & that I shall be able to pay you before this new debt will be contracted. . . .

Friday night.—We seem to have regain'd our Credit by giving Tea to all their (Ansons') party last night, siting by their Commerce table & inviting Winkfields to dinner to-day. Ld Vernon & ye Bishop of Peterborough both flirted with me so much yesterday that you w^d not have known which to be most jealous of. But it is now clearly decided for the Lawn Sleeves for I have been Shabby & not appear'd to-day, and Ld V. departs with the Ansons to-morrow. Nelly is at this instant with a fine Riot in ye Winkfields' Parlour hearing Mrs. Fox sing. They invited me & gave broad hints that my parlour was ye best Room but I had no notion of turning myself out for them & am really not equal to any Jollity to-night. . . . If pretty well on Sunday & ye day is fine shall after Church (or rather service) set out for Sheffield & return on Monday ready I hope to begin drinking & Bathing on Tuesday & (if it pleases God) to pursue it steadily without further interruption till all my Ill humours & bad Qualities are wash'd away. . . . I observ'd in the Card Room last night 6 or 7 very handsome genteel looking young men really above ye common stamp, but not a Name amongst them, where can they come from? Our great boasts now are Sir

George & Lady Coke & Sir George & Lady Barker. Are not these last ye People that had your house? They seem charming vulgar. . . .

Saturday night Oct. 6th.—Great news, a fine Paris Coach with Glass Pannels arrived containing Mr. Fitz Morris 2nd Son to Ld Shelburne, his Lady, her Sister, both pretty Women daughters to Ld Inchiquin with a most prodegious train of attendance, Led horses, side saddles & baggage up to ye top of the Coach. What an Event! What will they do here? Mrs. Winkfield says they are the most shewy pompous people in ye World. . . . If it is fine . . . we expect great entertainment in ye Drive (to Sheffield) for we go thro' ye whole of Middleton Dale which is one of ye great Lyons of ye Peak & Ned says by far ye most beautiful Rocks he ever saw.

Sunday morning. . . . Y^e Day charming and am going to prayers & then set out for the Beautiful Rocks at Middleton Dale. . . . Prayers over, Chaise at ye Door & Sun Shining. I wish you was going with us even though you sh^d put a Check to my extravagance. Adieu, adieu.

Monday night 8 o'Clock.—Just two hours since we arrived safe & well from Sheffield, the Weather made on purpose for us, the Road very even & good & the scenes more tremendously beautiful than any I ever saw before in England. I suppose we went about 2 miles nearer ye Gods than we sh'd have done owing to their not telling us to take a Short turn which was to Lead us down to Middleton Dale. Instead of that we kept on the great Sheffield turnpike which carry'd us up to ye top of a mountain where there was a sort of Plain if one may be allow'd to call it so, all black Rock & Ling, the Wildest place I ever beheld, at ye end of which is such a prospect open'd as makes my head turn to think on. I was sometime before I durst carry my Eye over ye Wild hills & Craggy Rocks at ye Bottom of which about 2 miles below ran ye Derwent; on ye other side of which ye hills were beautifully cultivated, plant^d & interspersed with Villages. We durst not sit in ye Carriage down ye steep parts of the Hill. Nelly indeed walk'd all the way, I daresay more than two miles, but my strength fail'd so I got into ye Chaise & came down very safe, William being indeed very careful. At the Bottom of the Hill ye Inn appear'd to our great Joy for we had no suspicion then of being out of our Road, but imagine our mortification when instead of the good fare we were made to expect at Middleton Dale we were behold with astonishment by ye Landlady & told there was nothing to be had but ye remains of a Joynt of Lamb which she & her family had dined upon. How did we then applaud ourselves for bringing with us a Large piece of our Excellent Venison Pasty & a pint of my Wine. On that we made a most hearty Meal, ye Serv^{ts} hash'd up ye Lamb & thought it excellent & all were well pleas'd to find we were only ten miles from Sheffield instead of 13 wch we should have been at Middleton. We got there before 6 had a good supper & charming Beds, were up at 7 & saw the Plated Manufactory through all its branches which is very curious indeed, made myself rich in conveniences which are to be sent to Arbury in about a month, came through Middleton Dale which is full as

beautiful as Ned described it & a much more level &
pleasant road than our *Black Sir William*, which I find
is ye name of that high Rocky Plain, but I cannot get a
reason why so call'd. Y^e People at ye foot of that hill
c^d give no acc^t at all, but ye Maid who waited upon us at
Middleton believed it was from Sir William a Conqueror
who fought there. Such a field of Battle is not usually
chosen, for it is entirely cover'd with pieces of Black Rock
most of them bigger than ye Conqueror himself who we
must suppose to have been a very great man. I am glad
we made him a visit now it is over but once in one's Life
is enough. . . .

Tuesday.—Another Heavenly Day & I have made y^e
most of it. Being inform'd that ye Chaise horses were a
Little tired with their Journey but that Mr. Lumber was
fresh I mounted my Pillion at this door, Rode up &
down hills manfully, then drank Water, bathed with like
Courage, Laying myself upon ye water according to your
directions & thereby getting as many duckings, I daresay
more than twenty for I have a wonderful alacrity for
Sinking. . . . Cork has been alter'd two or three times
& now does everything well but keep me above Water.
God bless you. Amen, amen.

Thursday evening Octr 11th.—There has been almost
an hourly arrival of Carriages yesterday & to-day. . . .
All this makes mighty Little difference to us. . . . We
have nothing to do with ye Owners of all ye fine Varnished
Coaches & Chaises. I have desir'd Nelly will send
Molly [1] a list of their Names tho' I am sure she will think

[1] Miss Mary Conyers, sister to Sir Roger's first wife, and now his tenant and near neighbour at Astley Castle.

we made them, but it is Literally true that ye most shewy people here are either Lightbodies, Littletails or Hardmans, & that we have not a speaking acquaintance with a Soul in ye Long Room except ye Bishop of Peterborough & Lady M. Fitz Morris who came up & introduced herself to me the first time I appear'd above in ye Civillest manner imaginable, as if glad to find somebody that she might venture to speak to. I told you wrong about her, she is ye only Child of ye deaf & dumb Lady Orkney & marry'd to ye Brother of the present Ld Shelburne. Y^e young Lady with her is a Miss Jones, a pretty Little inocent Welch Girl who yesterday entertained ye Bishop of Peterborough with a very naïve & ridiculous acc^t of her manner of Bathing & of standing upon her head in attempting to swim. . . .

Nelly Mundy writes the next letter for Lady Newdigate, who was suffering from the effects of one of her favourite emetics.

Buxton Oct. 14th.—I know I have not the least Chance of making myself agreeable to you, for you will run your Eye over the whole Letter not to be able to find a Line of Hetty's writing & then take an Aversion to me & everything I say. Confess fairly, is not this true? [Then follows an account of Lady Newdigate's amateur doctoring.] . . . You may conclude all is well and that there is a fair prospect of my restoring the dear Prioress [1] to you the middle of next week with improved health & looks. . . . This is a bad sixpenny worth. I wish I cou'd have made it better, but if I was to attempt giving you a pretty

[1] Arbury was built on the ruins of Erdburie Priory in the sixteenth century.

account of Friday night's Ball—old Gentlemen of 70 dancing with young Miss's of 16—I know you w^d not attend to a word of it. . . .

Lady Newdigate resumes:

Tuesday evening Octr 15th.—I need not employ a deputy to-night thank God, for I really feel able to thank you for two charming Letters & to answer them from Beginning to End, but I shall not be let to try ye strength of my Brains so far having in fact been much worse than I intended & promised to be when Nelly answered for me on Sunday night. . . . As my nerves & spirits were too much agitated to let me sleep I thought about 2 o'Clock it w^d be a wise act to take 3 of the opium pills. These seeming rather to increase my restlessness I supposed the quantity was too small & at four took 2 more. Still prepossessed with ye Idea & recollecting that Jebb in his very last letter desires me not to be afraid of them but to take them whenever particularly agitated, I thought I might go on taking two every two hours till they procured sleep & proceeded as far as number nine, when (providentially perhaps) my Courage fail'd me. No Sleep came but my Head was confus'd and I was sick. In this situation Nelly found me & when she heard what I had done had sensations which I believe it w^d not be very easy to describe, which however she endeavour'd to conceal for fear of hurrying me, took all possible pains to prevent noises, suffer'd nobody to speak or come near me but to give me what I wanted, & so I dosed on ye whole day & was in hopes ye effects of ye opium w^d have gone off without further Consiquence, but violent sickness, nervous sinkings & Cold Sweats came on towards evening. I knew Nelly w^d be terrify'd to death if she knew of it so I sent privately for Mr. Buxton ye Apothecary who I suspected w^d be allarm'd at the situation he found me in & therefore before I gave him my hand assured him I was not dying & told him what I had done, for which he has several times thank'd me for he says my Pulse w^d have surprised him greatly. He gave me a strong Nervous draught which had a speedy good effect. . . . My own folly about ye opium I must greatly regret and am so truely penitent that I hope neither you nor Nelly will scold me.

Here is St. Luke, ye 1st day that was fixt for our Meeting & it brings a Hamper of good things, Venison & Partridges sweet as possible, Pears & Pines in perfection, *Rouleaux* never out of season, a draught which I have given Nelly to put upon ye fire or Dunghill as she pleases, but first made her give me a rec^t for it, that it may be entirely her own affair. You may say what you will of not fearing my extravagance, but I have certainly made you believe that I sh'd lay out a very large sum in these same shim-Shams that have produced such fine argumentation on both sides or you w^d not have thought me in danger of remaining here in pawn after sending me with fifty guineas in my Pockett & last week sending me fifty more, but such Game must always be sweet & the more as it is a proof that you have a real desire to have me back again with all my follies and notwithstanding our *sad* differences in opinion. Indeed it is high time for we have been parted till we can't understand each other at all. I never c^d have ye most distant thought of your wishing to interfere in or even to know anything of my Private expences ; no one word or Action of your Life c^d give birth to such an Idea. You therefore must have hash'd & mangled ye meaning of my fine sententious harangue in a most Cruel manner. . . . You accuse me of mistaking your Meaning in a former occasion. I do not think I misunderstood one word, but your fancying I did had a mighty pretty effect. I would not erase a single line of all you say upon that subject for ye world tho' I agree with you that it is too trifling for the honor that has been done it, but as long as it *was honor* let it receive a return in kind.

Friday.—What machines we are ! I have been riding, Bathing, *swiming* & *sinking* without Cork in as bold a Manner as before my Illness, have ate a good dinner & feel inclined if I finish my Post in time to go up & peep at ye Ball which is to be this evening. . . . If you approve of my scheme of setting out after I have drank ye Water & Bathed on Wednesday it will be little more than an airing for me & ye horses & I shall gain a day & without hurry or fatigue be at Arbury to make your Coffee on Thursday. With what pleasure I think of that event I leave to your Justice to determine. . . .

From Nelly Mundy on the same sheet :—

Now I come in a Moderate way, neither presumptuously covering a whole sheet nor sneakingly squeezing myself into my Ld Bathurst's wig. If this Dear Soul has not given a *very* good account of herself she is a vile Wretch . . . if she continues to go on at the same rate till Thursday I shall not be ashamed to deliver up my Charge. I heartily wish I c^d do it in person but that is impossible. On Thursday I must infallibly be in Town.

... Adieu my dear Sr Roger, may you and y^r Cara Sposa meet in health & spirits & long enjoy an ample share of both those valuable Articles. ...

N. M.

The last letter of this series is evidently written by Lady Newdigate after receiving Sir Roger's answer to her letter containing the account of her hazardous experiment with the opium pills.

Sunday 21st Oct^r.—. . . What shall I say for giving you that Cruel Allarm for you was more hurry'd than your words bespoke you. *I must kneel down & Cry*, it is ye only thing to be done. . . . How good you are about my staying & your coming to me & how many pretty things you say! my Pen cannot thank you but my heart does. . . . I shall have a better way of conversing with you before to-morrow night ; any way I shall see you in a few hours after you receive this. . . . You seem to think I have been quacking myself. Indeed my dear Soul I am very certain & the recollection gives me pleasure that I have not taken, nor done a single thing in regard to my own health but what you w^d have approv'd & recommended, except ye Opium pills. . . . It is indeed a great mercy that I was not a greater sufferer. I am truely thankful for it & now I have confess'd my sins in full we'll neither think nor talk any more on the subject. . . . No more Letters from me.

P.S. from Nelly Mundy:

How very Ill poor little *I* am used kick'd quite out & not allowed room to explain of the Saucy Creature's barbarity. Indeed I durst not say much for she looks quite stout enough to knock me down.

CHAPTER IV

1782–1785

> Captain Wybrow always did the thing easiest and most agreeable to him from a sense of duty; he dressed expensively because it was a duty he owed to his position; from a sense of duty he adapted himself to Sir Christopher's inflexible will, which it would have been troublesome as well as useless to resist, and being of a delicate constitution he took care of his health from a sense of duty. His health was the only point on which he gave anxiety to his friends; and it was owing to this that Sir Christopher wished to see his nephew early married, the more as a match after the Baronet's own heart appeared immediately attainable.—Mr. Gilfil's Love-story.

WE begin this chapter with one of Lord Bagot's[1] cheery letters, announcing the inopportune arrival of his second son (afterwards the Bishop of Bath and Wells) at a country inn.

Saracen's Head, Daventry: Nov. 22, 1782.

DEAR SIR ROGER,—However awkard the Place I am happy to tell you my Wife was *here* this morning ab^t six o'Clock safely delivered of a fine Boy, & that she and her Child are both as well as possible. She was attended by Kerr of Northampton who always attends Mrs. Chester, wants no assistance & [she] is much more comfortably & quietly accommodated than you wo'd think it possible to be in an Inn.

When I made her excuses to Lady Newdigate that she did not dare visit her for fear of making her visit a month long, I little thought she wo'd have spent a month so near her at an Inn. If I co'd have dined & spent my time in

[1] William, first Lord Bagot.

your magnificent Library at Arbury I sho'd not have regretted my confinement, nor cared tho' her Ladiship had ordered the Maids to wash the Hall every day,—but neither must I regret it now but have every reason to thank Providence for the great dangers we have escaped & the security we are in now & the comforts we have to what they may [have been]. . . .

Yours most affec^{ately}
BAGOT.

In the spring of 1783 Lady Newdigate was in London for a short time in March and April, without Sir Roger, who had been called home on business. It was a time of some excitement in the political world, being the eve of a general election, and Hester in her daily letters to her husband takes pains to send him all the reports that reached her. She was also especially interested in the Derbyshire election, her brother, Ned Mundy, being considered one of the most popular candidates for that county.

In the following letters Lady Newdigate often mentions her Italian music master, by name 'Motta,' said to be the original of Sarti in 'Mr. Gilfil's Love-story.'

Tuesday March 23rd, 12 o'C.—I am waiting for Motta. . . . When Motta is gone I drive to Smithfield. . . home to dress & to ye Opera at seven, it is to be wonderfully shewy & the last Dance ye best, so we must see it out which perhaps may keep me too late to add a Word when it is over.

The next letter from Hester is begun in the handwriting of Mrs. Francis Newdigate. She was the wife of Sir Roger's cousin [1] and a daughter of Ralph Sneyd, of Keele. Lady Newdigate often writes of her and her husband as 'the little News' and of her as 'the Little Woman.'

I cannot my dear Sir let you remain *in ignorance* as to pollitecks, therefore have seized the last moment of the

---

[1] Francis Newdigate was an elder brother of Charles Parker's, who had taken the name of his maternal uncle on succeeding to his estates in Derbyshire and Notts.

Parlement to get a frank that you may have my intelligence gratis, for fear you sho'd think it was spight made me write *because I loose my wager.* The King is now gone down to the House to prorogue the Parlement which expires to-morrow & I am apprehensive that finding yourself *right* in this particular you may be induced to espouse Mr. Mainwaring's cause in Middlesex in preference to Mr. Bing, therefore I think it *right* to inform you Mr. Mainwaring is the son of a bricklayer & I hope you will not make me the same answer I have just had from Mrs. Conyers that it was better than *being the son of a gun.*

I know you will be very sorry to hear Lord Thurlow's house was broke open last night & the villains are got clear off with *the great seal.* It is a very extraordinary accident. *I am not superstitious* but surely it looks a little ominous. Lady Newdigate continues charmingly well & I know writes to you to-night, therefore I shall leave everything for her to tell but what relates to the *good* of the nation. I am affraid Sir Edward Littelton means to propose himself for Staffordshire & I am assured you are gone *to Canvas* Warwickshire. I am going to dine with Mr. Tollemache who I hear means to oppose Sir Robert Cotton in Chesshire & am to spend the evening with Mrs. Cornwallis. After all the pains I have taken to put you right it is unnecessary to assure you how much I am

      Your sincere friend,

Bedford Square: F. NEWDIGATE.
 ye 24th of March.

I shall send this & my frank open to Lady Newdigate knowing her unfortunate jealousy.

Lady Newdigate writes on the same sheet:

For fear Franks sh'd be charged I (Hester) will not add another sheet. The Little Woman tells you very true, The Seals are certainly stolen & not yet recovered. £100 in cash & a few rusty swords taken with them. Y^e King has prorogued ye Par^t till ye 5th of April. . . . Mrs. Newdigate is just come in & is very Angry to see me writing in her Letter. She says you'll think I sh'd have written a Whole Sheet if she had not. To convince her I have said all my say will wish you good night. . . .

Thursday night 25th March.—Ned's mind is so engaged about Election affairs that he could not sleep. Almost every Derbyshire Man except himself is gone down & one report says Curzon will come in without opposition; another that he will decline; a third that Ld Tamouth will be a Candidate; a 4th that Frank Burdett will be unanimously chosen. Ned is evidently anxious about the Event, therefore we have encouraged him to go down immediately & accordingly to-morrow at 6 in ye morning he sets off. We have persuaded him to go by Nottingham to see how Matters stand with his friend there. He told me he was canvass'd yesterday by one of ye younger Sheldons for his brother Ralph for Warwickshire & that his Answer was that he sh^d not take any part unless Sir R. N. interests himself; in that case he sh^d do his utmost for ye Person he espouses. He says Holbiche, (I beg his Pardon for not knowing how to spell his Name) Adderley, Sheldon, some other Person & the two present Members all declare they will stand, but perhaps you may know better for this is common report. Ld Feilding desires me to tell you that Mr. Manwayring opposes Bing in Middlesex & he hopes will carry it. The Seals are not found. Everybody supposes they were not Stolen by Common Rogues & that it must be done to answer some Gambling purpose as it is well known that many thousand pounds were depending on the day of dissolution. If it has delayed ye Proclamation for a Dissolution & answer'd their Vile purpose it will be grievous. . . .

Monday night 29*th March*, 9 *o'Clock*.— . . . A Letter from Trumper to say you may have a Cock Pheasant & 3 Hens for 4 Guineas, that is 1 Guinea less than ye Price in Town. Trumper says that this man sold 50 Pheasants that he rear'd last year to a Bird Man two months ago for 40 Guineas & that he is well assured you will not get them anywhere Cheaper than he offers them. He has promised ye Man an Answer on Thursday, but he cannot have yours before Saturday. Lyons is in search of pheasants for Ned, has been to all ye Bird Shops & they ask him 2 Guineas for Cock Birds & 1 for hens. . . . You seem to be hanging & transporting at no small rate. I hope you'll leave none but honest People in our Quarter.

Thursday April 1*st*.—Fox they say will be Chose for West^r & Sawbridge for ye City. Ld Denbigh looks blank upon it. He bids me tell you that Mr. Manwarring is proposed by Mr. Woods' son in Law & that Wood, Clitheroe & all your old friends are very active for him, & he hopes you will write immediately to your Steward to signify your Wishes for Mr. Byng is very importunate. There is a fine story coming out against Fox, proofs of bribery when he was in place. So Baker is kick'd out of his Borough & Genl Conway went down (to St E^d Bury I think) with full assurance of success 'he had served them in two Par^{ts} & hoped they would re-elect him.' He was answered that for that reason they were determined not to have him; w^{d} take any body else that ye Duke of Grafton pleased to send. He sent young Fitzroy Ld Southampton's son & he is Chose.

Ned writes word that Coke will come in again for Nottingham & that at present there is no appearance of Contest for the County of Derby. A Mr. Mac Namara or some such sounding name is gone down to oppose Booth Grey at Leicester & they say Sir S. Gideon to Coventry.

Friday.—To-night Fox lags behind but I suppose there is no Judging . . . Ned writes word that Derbyshire is asleep, no County Meeting called or likely to be unless an opposition is declared. There is no doubt of his coming in if he w^{d} spend a Little Money, but he wisely determines not to do that & therefore must wait ye Event. I must write a line to him so good night.

Mrs. Newdigate told me this evening that Ld Thurloe told her Ld Fielding had got the Treasurer's Staff. I suppose then Ld Guilford has resigned upon ye Queen's dismissing his grandson North who was his secretary. You remember that he rode behind Fox's Chariot; when the Queen was told of it she sent him word she did [not] like to be waited on by other People's servants & had no further Occasion for him. Mr. Howard, Lady Effingham's second son is appointed in his place. . . .

This letter was missent to Stafford, and only reached Sir Roger on his return to London a few days later. He seems to have complained of this gap in his wife's correspondence.

Lady Newdigate's last letter before his return was sent by hand to meet him on the road.

Fearing you must be late my Dear Life I have sent both your Men to guard you. God grant you may arrive safe & well. . . . The Post on Tuesday brought the News of my Brother's being a Candidate declared for ye County of Derby. . . . I have not neglected you either out of Idleness or forgetfulness, & I won't allow you to say such a thing even in Joke. I have had a multitude of things in my Head & upon my hands, all which you shall know. God bless you.

Mr. Mundy was duly returned to Parliament by his County at this election. Possibly he would not have been as anxious for the compliment paid him had he foreseen how costly the honour would prove. No doubt the position of a Member of Parliament in the last century was reckoned a higher prize than in the present day. The members of the House of Commons were fewer in number and more equalised in social status than now. The prestige they enjoyed was higher and their privileges were more numerous, not to mention the political influence that could be exercised, or the prizes that might be extracted by due pressure on the party to which individual members belonged. On the other hand the expenses of an election were enormous, and, if a contested one, almost ruinous.

Mr. Mundy had been warned against this danger when he came of age in 1771. He has preserved an excellent letter of advice written to him by the Lady Denbigh[1] who seems to have taken a motherly interest in the family at Shipley after they lost their own parents in 1767.

DEAR S^r [she writes],—Will you allow me to presume so far on the Priveledge you have granted me of calling you my Son, as to offer you a few Words of such Advice as is dictated by the sincerest wishes for your Happiness—which will almost entirely depend on your

[1] Mary, Countess of Denbigh, wife of the sixth Earl, and daughter and co-heir of Sir John Bruce-Cotton, Bart.

first setting out in the scene of Life you are now entering upon.

She then goes on to urge ' Religion' upon him as 'the only solid Foundation for real Worth & the only Defence against the Attacks of Vice,' and continues by warning him severally against the dangers of 'Gallantry,' 'Gaming,' and 'the society of thoughtless uninformed young men.'

Finally she gives her opinion on the evils of 'Electioneering' as follows :

There is a Branch of Expence almost as dangerous as Gaming & perhaps more immoral from the Perjury, Drunkenness, & other Vices which usually attend it. I mean Electioneering. The Honor which a Seat so obtain'd can confer is certainly not worth the Purchase. The Man who has no farther aim in hurting his Fortune than to be a Member of Parliament is a Fool. He who means to repair it again by selling his Vote—is a Knave; and considering the little Dependance to be plac'd on Ministerial Promises & the Fluctuations which for several Years past have attended Ministerial Power, probably will find himself in the End a Fool also. . . .

Mr. Mundy, unfortunately for his immediate successors, disregarded this sage advice, and when the tempting prize was set before him, could not bring himself to decline the honour of a seat in Parliament. In the end, thirty-nine years of parliamentary life proved so costly that he all but ruined his family and had to sell three estates to pay election expenses.

Later in the year Mr. Mundy lost his wife, who had been in delicate health for some time. The visit to Lisbon had not the desired effect, and after a lingering illness, she died at Brighton in November 1783. She left five children, four of them boys and one girl, named Fanny, after herself.

In the following summer Lady Newdigate paid one more short visit to Buxton, this time not on her own account, but to establish her sister Nelly there, who had been seriously ill. They travelled together from Arbury, accompanied by their motherless niece, Fanny Mundy, and made a resting place of the empty, melancholy house at Shipley on their way to Buxton.

Shipley 10 *o'Clock Tuesday.*—We got to Burton at ½ past one, Derby by three, had an excellent dinner . . . order'd our Chaises to proceed to this Place which we reach'd before 7 in a dismal misty Rain, the Hatchment over the door, forlorn state of every Room etc. made it really a melancholy scene. I rejoyced I was with ye dear Nelly but she appear'd to bear it better than any of us. Fanny shed a few tears at first coming in but the Joy of finding herself again at Shipley soon brighten'd her up & Nelly set herself to business. . . .

It is well we came for Lyons could not make ye Upholsterers believe my Brother w^d come down till Par^t broke up, so there is not a Room paper'd nor bed up. . . . We slept in the old Nurseries as we found they had been constantly lain in. . . . I have sent James forward for a pair of horses from Ripley for ye Maids chaise & we shall put my Brother's 4 to my Chaise which I think will draw us in two hours to Matlock. . . .

Buxton, Wednesday night.—I thought it better to stop at Matlock . . . & after a good Dinner & a walk about a ¼ of a mile up ye Hill came to a place call'd the Temple house ye most Romantic beautiful spot I ever beheld where Just ye number of Beds we wanted were vacant. There we drank our Tea & sup'd upon Strawberries brought from Shipley & Lay in as Clean Beds & in as quiet a house as possible. I should have told you the Principal houses were all full, & Mighty Smart Beaus & Belles walked by our Lodgings. I ask'd who they were & was told that there was nobody of *very great account* but Mrs. Lee of Chester. We were told that Buxton Hall ran over . . . so we thought it prudent to be out early. Before 7 were in our Chaise made a short Breakfast at Bakewell & at ½ past 11 arrived before ye Hall where 8 Post Chaises & Coaches full of Company were waiting to know if they could have admittance.

As soon as ye Mistress (who by the by is new to us all) c^d be got at I made James announce who we were, which procured us an Audience & we were requested to sit quietly in our Chaise till ye Companys were sent off. We were then shew'd into our old Blue Parlour which we learnt belong'd to Ld Keppell who is absent for a day or two. Here we sat a full hour when the Lady return'd with assurances that she had done impossible things for us, had procured us very tollerable Beds in a house at ye top of the hill for this night & that she has very great hopes she shall be able to take us in to the house tomorrow. The Maids have been all over the Place to-night & say there are no lodgings nearer than ye top of ye Hill & that those we are to sleep in to-night are Clean but very Paltry. I hope we shall have some changes before Saturday or I really do not see how I can possibly leave poor Nelly. . . . We have leave to sit in L^d K's parlour which is a happy circumstance. We are told of 4 L^{ds} & 7 Baronets that are com^g as soon as they can have lodgings.

Thursday night.—Keppell for Ever! If his Lordship

had not been so kind to absent himself at this time we Litterally sh^d not have had where to put our heads. We had a most Miserable hole to sleep in last night, but by great exertion, Bullying, Coaxing etc. we have obtained to Sleep to-night in a tollerable two bedded Room in this house. . . . I think ye only thing I can determine is that if you do not see me at Arbury before, to send the horses to Burton on Monday morning. . . . Supper calls, Adieu.

Oh I am glad you are not here. We were too hungry to go to bed supperless, & they w^d not let us sup in the Keppell, so we made part of 70 people at least, Noisy, Hot, & very disagreable, but thank God I am finishing my Letter in a very comfortable Looking Bed Room. It is large & clean but will be dismal by daylight for ye only Window there is is too high to see out of, and against a dead wall. However, by comparison it is a Paradice. Once more Adieu.

The next batch of letters of any interest were written by Lady Newdigate from London in May and June 1785. Sir Roger had gone back to Arbury, leaving his wife behind for another ten days. She seems to have been occupied with a course of music lessons from her Italian master, Motta, and also with an embryo love affair of Charles Parker's, in which both she and Sir Roger were greatly interested. The young lady in question was one of the three daughters of Lord and Lady Howe, presumably the eldest, as she is spoken of as 'Miss Howe.'

Tuesday May 24th.—I do not feel happy in the Idea that you are getting farther & farther from me every Minute. . . . As soon as you was gone I gave up my head to be tortured by Mrs Hood, then came Motta & stay'd above 2 hours. He remarked that Charles was distrait & so he was. I think him thoroughly taken in.

Whilst he was singing before I came down Miss Howe came in & was taken into ye drawing Room where I found her much entertained with hearing Duets between Ch^s & Motta behind the Curtain for they knew not that she was there. She came with an offer to me of Lady Howe's Box & Ticketts for to-night, & to ask me to dine with her on Thursday, neither of which I agreed to. . . . Miss Howe made me a very short visit, seeing I was engaged with Motta. . . . God bless you, take care of yourself for you was not well. I wonder how I c^d be so silly to let you go without me. I am sure it cannot answer to me, if it is to be the music of the spheres. . . .

Wednesday 25th 2 o'C.—. . . Our Ball was ye prettiest thing I ever saw & the girls all so happy it did one good to behold them. They danced alternately Minuets, Cotillions, Country Dances & figure dances from 7 till 12, then went down to an Eligant supper of ye inocent kind in ye great Room below. When we old ones had admired them some time we were invited to seat ourselves at a Table, a kind of Horse Shoe, which fill'd ye Little Room. . . . Y^e folding doors between the Rooms were taken away & the Appearance was indeed beautiful. At one o'clock ye Company broke up & ye Bartons brought me home. . . . We have changed our day for Kensington to Monday next, so I have just writ to L^{dy} Howe to say we will dine with her to-morrow.[1] If that produces an invitation to my Lodger [Charles] I shall think we are *en train*. I have taken occasion to mention

---

[1] It seems to have been then considered a compliment between friends when they offered themselves to dinner. This meal took place usually in the course of the afternoon and did not interfere with evening and supper engagements.

Mad^lle to Almost everybody I have been Company with since you went, in order to hear what people thought of her & they are unanimous in her praize. They say she is the most unaffected unassuming, properly behaved, best natured Girl in London. We talk of having another representation of our *Ombres Chinoises* on Friday. . . .

Answer from L^dy H.: 'Have you? yes to be sure & pray tell Mr. P. that I shall be glad of his Company, tho' my Lord dines out. . . .' Mrs Walsingham tells me that ye Dean of West^r has very few places this year allotted him & that it is a great favor & great Luck to have ye offer of one. . . .[1]

Thursday.—. . . Charles is not my Lodger yet. I believe not till to-morrow. Poor fellow he recollected an Engagement with Mrs Stead to ye Poles for to-day which obliged him to decline ye tempting Party at ye Admiralty [Lord Howe's]. I fancy that Circumstance has put him out of Spirits, for he call'd me aside after Breakfast to desire I w^d not give the hint before agreed upon, for upon thinking it over he was sure it could not do, & therefore it was best to drop all Ideas of the kind. I beg'd him not to be so despairing, but he made me promise to do nothing to-day. . . .

I call'd upon Ld Denbigh last night, found him in an earnest fit of the Gout; he was so happy to see us & beg'd us hard that we w^d play at whist with him to-night. That we promised & now I am sorry we did for Lady Howe has sent word she does not go out this evening & wishes us to stay. . . . I shall be too late for Lady Howe's dinner if I add more.

[1] For the performance of Handel's *Messiah*.

From Molly Conyers, sister to Sophia, Sir Roger's first wife

. . . My Lady & Nelly are up to the Ears in Angels & Devils preparing for a Grand Shew to-night with hardly time to get ready so I am permited to be Secretary. . . . Lady N. bids me say they had a very Pleasant Party yesterday at the Howes, staid till near 9 & then went to joyn Ld Denbigh's party, who was very much obliged by it; he is still in the Gout. . . .

From Charles Parker

Now they give me the Pen while the Ladies go to dress. We have heard of you at different Stages on the Road & this morning from Arbury. . . . I wish you was here for more reasons than one. There is a report that the Trent & Mersey Bill would still be thrown out in the Lords if the Matter was rightly understood, & the grounds of it explained to the Chancellor. Ld Weymouth is not awake or he might do much, but his Agent can do nothing & even Ld Uxbridge in his own Cause wants an Adjutor.

From Lady Newdigate

Our figures etc. are all finish'd, I am dressed & expecting my Company every minute. Charles has invited Mrs Foley & her Children, Nelly, Lady Anstruther & Miss, & Molly sends for ye Middletons from Kensington so we shall have a numerous audience. . . . Lady Howe has just sent us her Tickets for ye Opera &

her Box for to-morrow. If we are not too tired when we come from Thames Ditton to dress we mean to make use of them. Indeed we get very dissipated. I hope I shall bring a more quiet Mind & Manners to Arbury.

Friday night May 27th.—Our performance has gone off vastly well & I gave ye Bartons, Fauquiers & Molly a Cold Chicken afterwards. We all parted Just as ye Clock struck twelve & are to be call'd at seven. . . . Our Audience consisted of very Old & very Young, Old Middleton, Old Fauquier, Lady Gray, Mrs Sloper, Mrs Cotton & about 12 Children all highly pleased. I will pack up our Scenes on Monday that I may not be ask'd to perform again.

Saturday night ½ past 9.—We have had a Charming Day. . . . Mrs. W. friendly as usual & vastly delighted with our admiration of her Place which is beautiful & extensive far beyond ye Idea I had conceived of it & the house is Charming, the Rooms pleasant, spacious & numerous enough for her family with every Convenience she can wish for & the whole in a Stile as peculiar to itself as our sweet Arbury. . . . We got back at a ¼ before 9 & I find myself more inclined to thank you for your letter than to make use of Lady Howe's Box & Tickett. Nelly also seems satisfy'd with ye Amusements of ye Day & Molly thought it right to return to Harley Street; so three of the Ticketts sleep in my drawer which is pitty. Y^e 4th Charles was very glad of. . . .

Nulla dies sine linea is a Law I must joyfully subscribe, particularly as you are also exact in ye observance of it. . . . You tell me nothing about my Bees, or of the works in Swanland, nor of my Pheasants having laid etc. Ld Denbigh shew^d me in writing ye state of his Poultry Yard, 37 Pheasant Eggs set under hens, 20 Turkeys hatch'd etc. etc. in ye same prosperous stile. . . . Ld D. is very earnest about flinging out the Trent & Mersey Bill in H. of L^ds. He says there is not a doubt of its being done if Ld Weymouth w^d exert himself. His reception of Nelly and me was really affecting. He thank'd us repeatedly with tears in his Eyes, said he was a poor deserted Old Man that nobody thought about[1] beg'd us to come & dine with him before I go down & when we came away Whisper'd Nelly that the Vis^ct had neither Call'd nor sent to enquire after him tho' he had sent Eades to tell him he was laid up with ye Gout. Nelly sat down & wrote to L^d. F. as soon as she got home. . . .

Sunday Just come from Church.—The Howes are gone out of town but return Monday or Tuesday. *Our* spirits are mended but ye Little we have had opportunity of saying on the interesting subject seems to indicate a desire to have no hint given at present. So far I think with him that he sh^d have good reason to believe himself approv'd, of which upon talking it over I do not find any certainty. He says he is sure she has no suspicion of his liking her. A discovery of that kind may change her behaviour to him. . . .

I shall write a fine sensible Letter I daresay for here are Charles & Motta singing. . . . Wednesday I shall take Leave of all London friends, Thursday spend in y^e

---

[1] Lord Denbigh had lost his wife in 1782, but within the year he remarried. The second Lady Denbigh was Sarah Farnham, widow of Sir Charles Halford, Baronet. She survived her last husband fourteen years, dying in 1814.

Abbey & I hope friday see Arbury. God bless you. I have written this Letter in such a Cat-headed way that you won't know how to begin or end.

Tuesday.—Nelly & Charles are gone to ye rehearsal at ye Abbey & I have been paying till my Hair stands on End. Motta's demand was frightful. He fairly made out between me & Charles 64 Lessons, which with Music we have had of him—songs transposed etc. came to £26. 5. 0. . . .

I have got my Ticket of Admission to the Deanery on Thursday, not to be there till pst 11. I shall come home from the Abbey, undress & pack up which will be no unpleasant conclusion. The Messiah is to be rehearsed on Friday & so many People are going to it to avoid a Crowd that they will infallibly make one. . . . We din'd with open Windows (at the Middletons) & walk'd between ye Showers which has given me Rheumatism in ye back of my neck and shoulders, but I hope that Flannell & ye strength of Mrs. Hood's arm will take it off. . . .

I have nothing new to tell you on the important subject. I hear they are come to town. I'll have a Little more conversation with ye Young Man before I make my Leave Taking Visit, & if anything is to be said will send & appoint a time or they may be out & disappoint us. . . . My Neck is very stiff and I prudently sit here quietly . . . these Sour Winds make every body Complaining except Nelly who is really stouter.

Wednesday.—I sent to enquire after Lady Howe's cold & rec^d for Answer that she had ye Rheumatism in her Back & was not able to come out but would be glad to see me at one o'Clock. Milly[1] carry'd me & we found a family party ; ye young Ladies all 3 making & dressing Hats & Caps for a Ball which is to-night at Mrs. Dundass's at Wimbledon—L^{dy} H. prop'd up with Pillows & lamenting that she must break throw her Rule & send them with their Aunt Mrs. Howe. No one named C. P. nor could I bring him in but by head & shoulders which I thought was better left alone. He will be mortify'd to learn that they are not to be at Ranelagh to-night. I talk'd to him seriously upon ye subject as we came from Wimpole St^r last night & he seems really not sufficiently sure of the Lady's opinion to hazzard an Opening to ye principals. He is quite certain she has no Idea of his attachment. I do think that sh'^d be the first step. He says he shall have few opportunities now of seeing her & seems to despair of ye affair advancing any further this year, or of their Situation being Eligible sh^d it take Place. They must, as I told him, Judge of that for themselves, but till he is satisfy'd of that & of her affections, I do not think I can with any propriety do anything. He says they have never yet met since he thought seriously on ye subject. Perhaps the 1st interview may point out ye road that is to be taken. . . .

This evening I shall come home in good time in order to be an Able person to-morrow. They tell me we have all sorts of Advantages & Agrémens in Lady Yates' Places, don't go into ye Abbey till Just before ye King Comes & can get out at any time. So I shall be in no fear of

---

[1] Her sister, Mrs. Barton. An echo of this name must have lingered at Arbury until George Eliot's time. One of this authoress's most attractive heroines is called 'Milly Barton.'

distress. ½ past ten, Harley Street. Lady H. Conyers is here & Matilda Just off to Ranelagh. I hear no news except that the King & Prince of Wales are reconciled. The Latter drops his prosecution & goes to ye Birth Day.

Wimpole Street 9 *o'C. Thursday.*—Just going home to finish payments & pack up & if possible get a good Sleep & be as well as I shall be happy when I meet you on Saturday. I got home from the Abbey just in time to send you a Verbal Message by Nanny—that I had heard delightful Music much at my ease & was pretty well. . . . Love from all here Adieu.

We hear no more of Charles Parker's incipient love affair with Miss Howe, and are not told if he ventured to put his fortunes to the test.

In any case he was quickly consoled, for in September of the same year (1785) he married Jane (always called Jessy), daughter of Sir John and Lady Anstruther.

Two of the three Miss Howes married two years later, in 1787. The eldest, Sophia, who became Baroness Howe on her father's death, married the Hon. Penn Ashton Curzon, and Louisa, the youngest, married the Earl of Altamont, afterwards Marquis of Sligo. Lady Mary Howe [1] remained unmarried. A few years later she became godmother at Charles Parker's request to his youngest daughter, who was named Louisa by Lady Mary's desire, after her sister, Lady Altamont.

After Charles Parker's marriage to Miss Anstruther he seems to have been openly acknowledged as Sir Roger's heir to the Middlesex property, and he and his wife made their home at Harefield Lodge.

[1] Lord Howe was advanced to an earldom in 1788.

CHAPTER V

1787–1788

> When the fact that Caterina had a remarkable ear for music and a still more remarkable voice attracted Lady Cheverel's notice the discovery was very welcome both to her and Sir Christopher. Her musical education became at once an object of interest. Lady Cheverel devoted much time to it, and the rapidity of Tina's progress surpassing all hopes, an Italian singing-master was engaged for several years to spend some months together at Cheverel Manor. —Mr. Gilfil's Love-story.

LADY NEWDIGATE'S next match-making excitement was on behalf of her brother, Edward Mundy, who had been left a widower with five young children in 1783.

In the summer of 1787 there was a possible match in view for him which excited the keen interest of all his immediate relations. The lady of Mr. Mundy's aspirations was Georgiana, widow of Lord Middleton and sister of James Chadwick, Esq., of Kirklington.

Lord Middleton having died without issue, the title passed to a distant cousin, whilst all his available property, plate and jewels he appears to have left to his widow. Lady Middleton had an only sister, Mrs. Whetham, who was also a widow with no family.

Whilst the courtship was in progress Lady Newdigate was summoned to Shipley, to give her sympathy and help in this desirable alliance. She writes to Sir Roger from Shipley on July 4, 1787:

We had a very hot drive to Aspley tho' we changed our plan and went to breakfast, but the coming back from two to four was insupportable. We saw a great deal of fine hay carry'd, this climate is forwarder than our upland Country. Willoughbys were much pleased with our

visit and make great enquiry after you. Y^e serv^t is returned from Kirklington [where Lady Middleton was staying with her brother, Mr. Chadwick] wth a very kind note accepting the offer so Mrs. Oliver, Nelly [Mr. Mundy's two sisters] & Helena [Mrs. Oliver's daughter] set out at 10 in ye morning for it is near 30 miles. We shall think it very hard indeed if no good comes of the sacrifize we make in dividing the sisterhood just now, but I flatter myself it will be forwarding the purpose I came for. Ned's spirits have risen greatly since this Plan was first [suggested] he seems much obliged to us all for giving into it. They will return to dinner on Friday & I hope to make My Dears Coffee on Saturday.

The scene is next transferred to Cheltenham, where Lady Middleton and Mrs. Whetham are staying, also a certain Fanny Willoughby, a member of the late Lord Middleton's family, whose good will on behalf of the suitor has been gravely doubted. Mr. Mundy's courtship of the fair widow seems to have made considerable progress, and he has with him an anxious and zealous sympathiser in his sister, Nelly Mundy. Mr. Mundy writes to Sir Roger from Cheltenham on October 19, 1787, as follows :

My dear Sir,—Yours and Lady Newdigate's Letters we have just received, and though we did not intend you should hear from us by this day's post, I cannot let it go without a few Lines from me to thank you both for your very kind Letters. Yesterday's post would inform you how happy we all are and with what generosity L^{dy} Middleton placed entire confidence in me. I must now assure you both that we are perfectly satisfyed F. Willoughby has acted the friendly part by me, and the appearances we observed soon after her arrival were produced by the fresh sensations you have heard of. The Joy she appears to feel is not such as could be put on if a long concerted plan had failed and she had been disappointed. Indeed her sincerity in this business cannot now be doubted, and I beg you will not only acquit her of any Deceit and Interestedness but endeavour to remove any Prejudices my sister Oliver may have conceived against her. We do not yet know what day we shall leave Cheltenham but you shall hear by Sunday's post. I hope everything will be fixed to-morrow.

God bless you all and thank you a thousand times for your goodness to me and anxiety about me. I hope very soon to introduce to you a sister you will not totally dislike. Nelly joins me in love to all. . . .

I am dear Sir,
Your affec^{ate} Brother & sincere friend
E. M. MUNDY.

Lady Newdigate we may believe never saw this letter, as she must have started for Cheltenham before it could have reached Arbury. Evidently Mrs. Oliver, who was at Arbury, was imbued with such grave suspicions of Fanny Willoughby's opposing influence that she induced her sister to leave with her for the scene of interest at once. They arrived at Cheltenham on Saturday the 20th, and Lady Newdigate writes to Sir Roger on Sunday the 21st:

What a lovely day we had for our journey! it was ye more agreable because I knew it would be Joy to you. Nothing c^d be more pleasant or prosperous than our progress. We got to Stow by one o'clock & was there advised to go by North Leach ye late Rains having made ye short Road almost impossible; another reason for not attempting it was that we c^d not get four horses. A pair brought us perfectly well to North Leach 9 miles and a fresh pair 11 miles to Cheltenham. So many people are now upon the wing from this place that ye place w^d not furnish more. We made an excellent Dinner upon our Cold Loaf & arrived here about ½ after four. They were sitting round ye table in a front room & upon the Carriage stoping flew into ye Passage, & seeing Mrs. Oliver get out concluded that poor Helena was worse and that she was carrying her to Bath, but on my appearing ye exclamations of Joy & surprise were very great. They had not the least expectation of my coming, seem'd overcome with pleasure & cry'd out, 'Oh how very good Sir Roger is to send you!' I ask'd Nelly if all went well, she said she hop'd so. Y^e Company we found was themselves, ye Bowdlers & Fanny Willoughby. Y^e Latter I had greeted *en passant* but did not pay much attention to her till we became seated when I observed a gloom & kind of embarrassment which I could not help observing to her, & told her she look'd as if she was not glad to see me. She try'd to shake it off as well as she could, but was evidently so struck that she c^d not recover herself, & in about ten minutes took her leave saying that Lady M. would expect her, that she w^d see us again before she went, that she must set off at three to-day if possible, as her brother w^d be waiting at an Inn for her about twenty miles from hence, but that she sh'd not go if L^{dy} M. was not better. *She* has kept house with a cold these two days & I am afraid will not be well enough to let us come to her to-day, for we have just sent & find she is not up. I don't find that anything goes wrong but yet we don't advance. Ned stay'd with us the whole evening which I enquired ye reason of and was told (at least understood) that Lady M. had desired he w^d not come last night. Upon further examination I learn that he was stop'd by F. W. who came as soon as she had Din'd & told him she knew it w^d be more agreable both to Lady M. & Mrs. W. [Whetham] that he sh'd not come. I have scolded him for minding her & advised never to take a denial but from her own mouth & to tell both ye Ladies that F. W. kept him away. I am certain that she trys to make Lady M. believe he has no real attachment for her. Ned observed how much she was struck at my coming & thinks she will not dare to go as long as I stay. I don't know what she fears from me unless she thinks that I see through her, & that she shall not be able to intimidate me as she does Ned & Nelly. They think she has an influence and are quite afraid of her. I won't offend her if I can help it, but I will put an end to misteries if possible, which will be disarming her entirely. Ned does not think that she means to be his enemy, but that she has some interested plan which she is trying to bring about & which makes her wish at present to keep back the business. I shew'd your letter to Bess [Mrs. Oliver] and Nelly; they are both much pleas'd and obliged to you for it. You bid me not shew it Ned, but I told him of it & consulted with him about sending it. He wishes it to be kept back if possible till F. W. is gone, if she goes to-day. If she does not I will deliver it the first time I am admitted. Ned will walk there from church & hopes to see her. He will tell her the reason of my coming & desire to know when I may wait upon her. Nelly is just come in with Blank Face again; she has been let in but finds all Cold, & she thinks with Anger in ye Countenance, & is all agitation, expecting that Ned will have his dismission, but I hope she frights herself unreasonably.

As the case stands, it is possible you may see me before Wednesday, or that it may be important my staying a day or two beyond that time ; therefore I think you had better not send for me; the difference of horses in this situation I am sure you won't think worth considering.

I must end or shall be too late for even^s 3 o'Clock Church, which we are going to, and Ned is not come home.

God bless you my d^r Life, Nelly makes me as great a fool as herself. My brains are turn'd round. I really think if this affair lasts long so, she will have a shaking Palsy. Lady M. is not well enough to see me to-day and Fanny W. does not go till to-morrow. I wish she may then.

This letter is enclosed in a larger sheet, on the inside of which is a short note to Sir Roger from Ned Mundy, headed 'Read the cover first.'

Cheltenham : October 21, 1787.

MY DEAR SIR ROGER,—Not five minutes ago I was made the happiest of mortals by receiving L^{dy} M.^{s} consent. God bless you and thank you for all y^r kindness. L^{dy} Newdigate is well & as happy as I am almost.

I am your happy & affec^{ate}
E. M. MUNDY.

The next letter is from Lady Newdigate, dated ' Monday 3 o'C. 22nd Oct.'

We have just had our presentation in form. *She seems very unwell but looks smiling & happy, & a more interesting Elegant Creature I never saw.* I gave her your Letter which she received very graciously; everything seems as we could wish, but that our poor foolish Nelly is sick. She was not able to go with Mrs Oliver & me to L^{dy} M. We laugh'd at her yesterday for Reading so Ill, but ye consiquence is too serious. She agitated herself so much that it gave her violent Complaint in her Bowels, which continues & she is feverish. Had she been well perhaps I might have surprised you before this Letter arrives, but as it is, I shall stay till Wednesday & be with you by Coffee time. Y^e Happy Man & Nelly hope to follow us in a day or two.

        Adieu, Ever, ever Y^{rs}.

Mr. Mundy's marriage was not long delayed. He writes to Sir Roger from Shipley on January 21, 1788:

MY DEAR SIR,—In return for your very kind Congratulations and good wishes which I thank you for most sincerely; I will tell you that I am the happiest creature on Earth, and impatient to introduce my dearest Lady Middleton to her relations at Arbury. She has kindly promised to pay you a visit whenever you like to receive us, and wishes to prevent Lady Newdigate coming through our very bad roads. We do not intend to stay more than one night or two at Middleton before we go to town or we could have had the pleasure of seeing you there. I mention Lady Newdigate's coming to Shipley alone because I know you dislike to go from home in Winter to any distance. If you could see us I think you would like us very well, so don't stand upon ceremony with us. We shall not undertake the Journey either with reluctance or fear of the roads I assure you. Lady Middleton desires to add her *Love* to you and Lady Newdigate and Compts to the News : Nelly is quite silent but I believe she has some Love for you all. I have a great deal and am your truly affectionate

Brother & Servant
EDW. MILLER MUNDY.

We hear of Lady Newdigate paying her first visit to Shipley after the advent of its new mistress in the following summer of this same year—1788. She had a second attraction to the neighbourhood at that time, being anxious to attend a grand musical performance which was to take place at Derby. She therefore stopped for a night or two at the county town, and was met by her relatives from Shipley, who had come in for the same object.

In the next letters we find the first mention of Sally Shilton, the little girl brought up and educated by Lady Newdigate on account of her beautiful voice. She was the original of Caterina, the heroine of 'Mr. Gilfil's Lovestory,' but was not of Italian parentage as the tale makes out. Report says that Sally Shilton was the daughter of a collier on the property, and Lady Newdigate's attention was first attracted to the child by hearing her singing whilst seated on the cottage door-step. She was taken to Arbury at an early age for the cultivation of her voice, and developed so much musical talent in addition to her unusual gift of song as to lead to ambitious hopes of her making her mark as a professional singer. Both Sir Roger and Lady Newdigate became much attached to the little girl, and as she grew up she was gradually promoted from the housekeeper's room to the drawing-room, where her musical gifts gave constant pleasure to her kind patrons and their guests. Lady Newdigate's former singing master, Signor Motta, was engaged to train Sally's voice, and seems to have spent much time at Arbury for this purpose. Her history will be unfolded in due course by Lady Newdigate's letters and one or two of Sally's own compositions. At the date at which we have now arrived—1788—Sally must have been about fourteen years old.

Friday 4 o'Clock Shipley.—We have just arrived about a quarter of an hour, & the first Dinner Bell is ringing, but as this is really the first Leisure Moment I have had since I enter'd Derby on Tuesday I must dedicate it to my Dear Life & thank him for ye very great pleasure he has procur'd me in this Jaunt, which has answer'd in every agreable light far beyond my expectations or even my hopes. I had a very pleasant Journey (barring the Idea of leaving you behind) & arrived at ye Nunnery at 6 o'Clock where my good old friend rec^d me with tears of Joy & of the most cordial kindness. We had just drank a quiet dish of Tea, when a Shipley serv^t arrived to say ye whole party w^d be with us in half an hour. Accordingly within that space ye Little Room was fill'd with (I thought) a tollerably well looking set, all well & joyous, glad to see me, wishing for you also and blessing you for sending me. They sat with us till our supper was ready & then departed to their Lodgings leaving the dear Nelly with us who is in perfect health. In the usual Stile she had (upon seeing a request in ye Daily Paper from ye Managers that the Ladies w^d not wear Hats or Bonnets either in the Church or Theatre) saved me a hurry by providing a Cap ready for me. The first performance was the Messiah. We call'd at Lady M.'s lodgings at half past ten and went all together. The Directors were waiting for us at the Door & handing us through the Crowd placed us all in y^e Mayor's Pew which had been kept for us. Ld Vernon & Mr Mundy in particular paid us y^e greatest attention, handed us out in y\ same manner & kept places for us in the Theatre, of which diversion I did not partake either Day; the 1st I had a little Headach & being told that it w^d be amazingly Crowded & hot, Nelly advised me to save myself, & their experience of y^e heat kept us all away y^e second evening. Indeed we thought ye Church & Assembly quite sufficient. As ye Latter was thought a necessary Compliment to the Town L^dy M. insisted upon going; it was stupid enough, but it pleased & we got back to our snug Lodgings before twelve.

Mara promised Harrison to sing her best & she really kept her Word. I never liked her so well; she was in high good humour & said she never sang in a Place that suited her Voice so well. Indeed, I had no recollection of its being so fine & spacious a Church. There were 1,300 People in it ye first day & many more the second & tho' ye Weather was very hot I cannot say that I was oppress'd. The Meeting was ye best as to Company that had ever been known in ye Town.

Our old friends were so good as to take in my 2 footmen & my Brother had bespoke stabling so my Serv^ts & Horses were well off, but many had no place to put their heads in. I hope you will receive your Horses safe and well. They have perform'd vastly well & all the Serv^ts have been as sober & attentive as possible. . . .

They wish to keep me [at Shipley] ye latest day which I have said positively is thursday; that neither my inclination nor Conscience can keep me longer as you have given me Carte Blanche. Therefore on that day if you think me worth fetching from Twycross, I will dine with you I hope & with all ye good people I left at Arbury. . . .

Motta sends Sally a Lesson to get against he comes. Tell her to practice it. We agree'd in a Whisper that there was not a singer at Derby equal to her. He seem'd disappointed that I did not bring her, but don't tell her so. She has I doubt not been gaining more at home & I hope amusing you & your Company. We are all very well but tired & sleepy as you will guess by this Letter. Mrs. Whetham leaves us to-morrow. Good night.

Shipley, Sunday night.—Though my last letter was writ in my Sleep, I hope it w^d convey my waking sentiments to my Dear Sir Roger which must ever be those of ye tenderest affection & gratitude. He w^d not I am sure be a little glad to find ye scheme he so kindly plan'd for my Enjoyment had so fully answer'd his wishes. I can now with certainty add that none of the party are the worse for it. We were all exceedingly amused but ye very pretty Attention paid me by so many friends & acquaintance, many of whom I have not seen for more than 20 years, gave me more than common pleasure, & made ye expence of Spirits ye greater. I think I never enjoy'd ye fresh air and a quiet drive more than I did from Derby to Shipley. We were all too much tired to stir out of ye house that evening. Lady M. had a bad headache & Mr. Chadwick who had ventured to ye Church performance both days was very unwell, but 2 nights sleep has set us all to rights.

Ned went a shooting yesterday morning & left a Charge that I sh'd not see any of ye New works till his return, so Lady M. drove me out in the Chair. We took a round & that shew'd us Shipley on every side, & the admiration that was bestow'd on its beauties & praises that seem'd involuntarily to break out every now & then of its *Owner* made 2 hours appear very short to me. We heard him shoot at a distance & were quite fidgetty that we c^d not get over ye brook that parted us. I think I never saw anybody's Countinance & manner express complete happiness so strongly.

In the evening Ned walk'd me into every Barn, Coachhouse, Stable round his New Walls, built & building. They seem well contriv'd & very convenient, I think you will approve. They talk of ye Great Room but nothing is done towards it, which Ned says is ye fault of his *Architect* [Sir Roger] who ought to have been here now & have form'd his plan upon ye spot.

In ye middle of dinner yesterday arrived Fanny Willoughby; she was at ye Musick at Derby, went on friday somewhere beyond Ashborn where she purpos'd staying a week, but on Lady M.'s telling her that I was going to stay some days at Shipley she dispatch'd an order to Aspley to send over her 2 Clavicellos [1] & they arrived about an hour before her. We play'd a good deal in the evening and Motta composed a very pretty thing that we perform'd admirably. Fanny went home to Mass to-day, but promises to return to-morrow & we have made Ned bring out his flute & he is to get it in order to play trios. Motta has compos'd a very fine bravoura song for Sally, which he fetch'd me to hear before we had been 3 minutes in ye house; tho' he is very happy here, he will I am sure be very glad to get to his little scholar. . . .

[1] A clavicello seems to have been an instrument of a composite character. It consisted of a violoncello with a keyboard attached to it. There is no specimen extant at Arbury, but one is represented in Romney's portrait of Lady Newdigate.

I don't believe I have mention'd ye dear Boys, they are all much grown & look vastly well; they were very glad to see me & Henry has ask'd several times why Sir Roger w{d} not come? Mrs. Whetham is, if possible, fonder of them than Lady M. is. They return to Eton on Wednesday.

We have been to Heynor Church, had a Charming Walk after Dinner till Tea & now the Bell has just rung to Prayers. . . . God bless you my dear Soul & keep you in health for ye sake of Yr truly affec{ate}

H. N.

CHAPTER VI

1789

For the next ten years Sir Christopher was occupied with the architectural metamorphosis of his old family mansion. . . . Though Lady Cheverel did not share her husband's architectural enthusiasm, she had too rigorous a view of a wife's duties, and too profound a deference for Sir Christopher, to regard submission as a grievance.—MR. GILFIL'S LOVE-STORY.

A YEAR later, in 1789, we find Lady Newdigate in London with her niece Fanny Mundy and her *protégée* Sally Shilton, but without Sir Roger, who had left Spring Gardens for Arbury before her. She appears to be detained for a time on more than one account. She proposes to attend the Birthday Drawing-room; Sally's music lessons have to be continued; whilst, lastly and principally, she is anxiously awaiting the first confinement of her brother's second wife. Lady Middleton is in London for this event, and established with Mr. Mundy in their Piccadilly town house.

Lady Newdigate's first letter home is dated 31st May 1789.

I am just come from Church my dear Love & at ye Altar have implored for Blessings on your head & for many returns of this day [1] more & more happy & accompany'd with all that your heart can wish. . . . Sally is very well

---

[1] Sir Roger's epitaph in Harefield Church tells us he was born on May 20, whilst in Archdeacon Churton's memoir he is said to have been born on May 30. Here we should be led to suppose his birthday was the 31st of the month. The only explanation for this confusion of dates seems to be that the 31st was the date of his first marriage to Sophia Conyers, and they may have kept this day as one of happy remembrance for so long that Sir Roger had forgotten his real birthday.

G

& her Voice Clear but not strong. That I hope will come, Motta does not doubt it.[1] He comes to both [Sally and Fanny Mundy] every day & they are studying a new duet for you. Lady M. is very good & desires me always to bring Sally, but it w^d interfere too much with her business as Fanny & I are great part of the day there, but she has Din'd there several times and I always take her when I go in an evening as Lady M. is delighted with their singing together, which they are studying to do without accompaniment, which is very useful & agreable & will make our Water Partys Charming. . . .

Monday 1st June.—Joy to us all, the anxiously expected Event is happily over. Lady M. was safely delivered of a fine Girl at 4 o'Clock this morning. She was in strong Labour from 6 o'Clock & had a very hard time indeed. When ye Child was born she was so exhausted that we were for several hours under great apprehensions for her safety, & the Doctor seems to intimate that if it had lasted any longer it might have been fatal both to Mother & Child—certainly to ye latter—for it was so long before it cry'd or shew'd signs of Life that we all concluded it dead, but thank God it squall'd at length with a Voice as strong as ever I heard Sally's. Mrs. Whetham, Lady H. [Howe] Mrs. Heywood & myself were with her ye whole time & could not be easy to leave her till eight o'Clock when her faintness went off & she fell into a sweet sleep. The Child eats like a Cormorant & is as promising as possible. A servant was sent express to Shipley for ye Wet Nurse ye Moment it was born, but one must be procured in ye meantime, for it's thought Lady M. will not

---

[1] Sally was about fourteen or fifteen at this date.

have milk for it which will be a disappointment. I got to Bed before nine & lay till near one but could not close my Eyes, my nerves have been upon ye stretch so many hours that it must take time to get them into a proper state for sleep which I doubt not they will be by an early hour this evening. Then the chance is that I sleep too sound & get ye headach. I have an invitation to dine to-morrow at Ld Bagot's but shall excuse myself on ye supposition that I shall not be fit to come into Company. I feel very tollerably well & all my attendant companions appear to be so. . . . I have fears for Mrs. Whetham only. I never saw a Creature suffer more from anxiety. I sh^d tell you that ye Instant we were summoned to Lady M.'s Room we were all Charging our Glasses to ye Brim, some with Wine & others with Water to ye Health of ye Day [Sir Roger's supposed birthday].

I sent Jessy [Mrs. Charles Parker [1]] our good news. She answers kindly that it makes her feel to have got rid of half her Burden. Poor soul, I wish she was in ye same state, with one little change perhaps she w^d say. The Little Girl is quite ye Welcome Guest in Picca^dilly.

I am going to eat my Mutton with my girls, and shall go early in ye evening to Jessy after calling in Piccadilly. My Bro. felt so happy that he did not know he was tired. I left him drinking Coffee & ordering his horse to ride out.

Be assured my dear Soul that I really am well, as a person can be who has work'd so hard and had no Sleep.

Tuesday 2nd June.—My Head is well to-day, but I feel

---

[1] Mrs. Parker was daily expecting her third confinement, and having had two girls, she much desired a boy.

my nerves very much shaken. The air has done me good. Fanny & I walk'd to Piccadilly & find Mother & Child going on well, but ye latter w^d have been lost without great attention. It had not slept for 14 hours when it was discover'd that ye temporary Wet Nurse they had hired had no Milk for it. Lady Howe & Mrs. Whetham were 6 hours driving about in search of a nurse yesterday,—fortunately found one with plenty of excellent Milk which ye Little Soul sucks with such glee it is quite delightful to watch it.

Many happy returns of ye day to us my Dr Love [their wedding day]. I thought as you did of its being ye 1st time we had been divided on its happy return since we came together. We will celebrate it old Stile with double Joy. . . . At this instant Rhodes enters with a petition. James Wagstaff has so exquisite a taste for London that he begs to stay another day to go to ye Birthday, for he hears that I am to be as fine as ye Queen & that he can never see so fine a sight as ye Ladies going to Court. I at first said positively *no*, we have trespass'd one day already & I thought you w^d not be pleased, but upon recollection that on a day of great rejoicing it was not possible to inflict mortification I call'd out Yes, Yes, in almost ye same breath.

I have had a note from Molly [Conyers] to say she hopes to get away from Sunbury to-day. If she comes & we feel both well in the evening, my Brother & I have laid a scheme to surprise & delight ye two girls with ye sight of all ye Decorations of the Spanish Embassador's entertainment which Lady Howe says surpass'd everything that has been or can be imagined. The girls know nothing of ye Matter, but after dinner we are to dress ourselves a Little Smart to drink Tea in Picc^{dilly} where we arrive at 8 o'Clock. My Bro. & George are to desire us not to get out of the Coach; we take them in a drive away to Ranelagh which we shall have to ourselves, but it will answer our purpose. Our party will be all Joy, we shall Drink Tea, walk about & before ye fine World arrives come away, for my Bro. will order ye Coach where to stand & we are to be at home by 12. If this takes place & answers my expectations of giving delight it will be better than all ye finery to-morrow.

I have got my Cap & all my things ready so shall dress without hurry—& I really do believe my gown will be ye most beautiful & Eligant. I daresay you'll have a description in ye Newspaper. I hope to set out on Monday 4 o'Clock. Molly just arrived, agrees to our Party, will take up her abode in our Garret & travel down with us. That settles everything, for I can leave Saml to go with ye goods & shan't have 2 men to attend us. Much love & good wishes from us all. Ever, ever Y^{rs}.

King's Birthday 10 *o'Clock, Wednesday 3rd June.*— We had a nice Party last night, walk'd about and saw very fine things much at our Ease; then drank our tea, after which Molly & I got seats & sent Fanny to Gallop round & round with her Father & Brother till 11 when we got our Coach up immediately & were in our own house before 12. There was a double Row of Coaches going to Ranelagh almost from ye Lock Hospital. By one or two o'Clock I suppose it w^d be so full there w^d be no stirring. What nonsense!

I have had a good Night & feel very equal to yᵉ fatigues of yᵉ Drawing Room, but I shall hate to have my pretty Gown torn to pieces, which I know it will be. I expect my hairdresser every instant & do not expect to get home before yᵉ post goes. I shall begin to prepare for my departure as soon as this Ceremony is over, for if all goes well in Piccadilly I have set my heart upon being with you on Monday evening & shall leave Samˡ as I told you to see yᵉ goods weighed & Loaded, unless you forbid me. . . . I must leave you for pride & vanity.

Adio Caro mio.

Friday 4 *o'Clock* 5*th June* 1789.—Two Lines you shall certainly have and two very satisfactory I hope you will think them. In yᵉ 1ˢᵗ place we are all well. Lady M. had a little uneasiness with her Milk yesterday, but all perfectly right to-day. I have no headach after my fatigues of Court but have been fagging since 8 this morning in order to dine with you on Monday which I think we may do from Dunstable, & as all paying & packing must be finished to-morrow if we are to set out on Monday, we may just as well eat a Chop after Church on Sunday & twirl down to Dunstable.

Jessy bold well for aught I know.¹ I am going to her this evening & we dine in Piccadilly. . . . Adieu.

Saturday 5 *o'Clock*.—Oh you tardy Mortal, not send your horses for me till 9 o'Clock on Tuesday morning! Why I shall have had a good Sleep at Arbury by that time. I have been packing & paying & paying & packing till I have a Broken back and Empty purse. In truth this long stay & the Birthday has made money run very

---

¹ Mrs. Charles Parker gave birth to a third daughter on June 14.

short, but I have made Ned supply me, & told him you will redeem me if he throws me into Prison. My mind at this moment stands thus. Finish all business, take leave of friends etc. to-night. Go quietly to Church in ye morning, set off at 2 with a Cold Loaf in our hands, proceed as far as we like, certainly to Dunstable, & I hope as certainly be with you before ye Dinner time. So if ye Blacks are not ready for me I shall growl. Heaven bless you and send us a Happy Meeting. Love to all.

Before these letters begin again Lady Middleton's short married life with her second husband had come to an end. Lady Newdigate was summoned back to London in great haste by the following letter from Mr. Mundy to Sir Roger.

MY DEAR FRIEND.—Long before this reaches you my Beloved Georgiana will be no more. She was taken with a Shivering yesterday morning and has been gradually declining ever since into the miserable situation She is now. Break this afflicting News to my dearest Hetty & Fanny [his daughter] and if you will do the kindest thing in ye world Give my dear Hetty leave to come to your
Afflicted Brother
E. M. MUNDY.

London: Sunday 4 o'Clock, June 28th 1789.

Lady Newdigate, with her ever-ready sympathy, obeyed this summons at once. She writes on the road from her first stopping place:

½ *past* 10 *o'Clock* [probably Monday, June 29, 1789]. This instant arrived at Stoney Stratford where I think it prudent to stop. I am well except a little Head Ach & much Heart Ach, both much increased with ye Idea of having left you in such an uncomfortable Melancholy way. Pray God keep you well & reward you for this kind Act to my poor distress'd Brother, who I am sure must feel himself incapable of Acting or he w^d not have ask'd you to have sent me. I found ye Roads very heavy & ye Ld Lieutenant of Ireland being gone by to-day I have had tired Horses for 2 stages. I am come to my new friend at ye Cock, have ordered a Chicken for my Supper which I shall eat in haste & get to Bed, in order to be out if I can at 4, which will bring me to town as soon as if I had gone on to Dunstable. . . .

Piccadilly, Tuesday 30th June 1789. 2 *o'C.*—I c^d not sleep after 2 o'Clock, so got out at 3 & was in Spring Gardens at 11. Just wash'd my hands & brush'd my Coat & came in a Chair to this Melancholy house. The porter flung open the Parlour door, but my legs trembled so it was some minutes before I c^d get so far. Ned & Mrs Whetham both fell upon my neck & we all were releaved by a flood of Tears before anybody c^d utter a word. Chadwick came into ye Room just after. They are all deeply distress'd but I think as far as I can judge pretty well in health & the dear little Inocent Cause of all this misery in a perfect state. I have just seen it in a sweet sleep. I wish'd also to have seen ye quiet sleep of ye poor dear departed Angel, but find she is already so very offensive that Lyons has just call'd me out to urge the expediency of nailing down the coffin. That being ye case I know not whether you might not think there may be something noxious in ye fumes, & have fears about me. I have not yet seen Ned except in ye presence of Mrs Whetham or Chadwick so can tell you nothing more. Lyons knows no more than that her Lawyer was sent for yesterday & came. He supposes with the Will but nothing has transpired, nor are any orders yet given but what were absolutely necessary. I am very well in health I give you my Word & my spirits will get quiet by and by, I don't doubt. I find a Letter from each of my Sisters which I send you. You will see that both have been seriously Ill and I doubt this News will overset them both again. Ned knows that Nelly had had a Violent Nervous Attack & therefore made Lyons write by the post only to Barton [Milly's husband] to break it them & to say he was sure you w^d have ye goodness to let me come to him; therefore he desired Nelly w^d not come. He desires me to say how deeply he feels your kindness to him. Indeed I do think as far as I can judge at present that some friend is absolutely necessary & I don't hear of one they any of them have in town.

Ned brings me a List of Letters to write for him so Adieu till to-morrow.

Y^{rs} Ever.

Spring Gardens, Wednesday 11 *o'Clock* 1*st July* 1789. I came home to a well-air'd Comfortable Bed between nine & ten & got some good sleep, but my head was so full of the melancholy business which I have taken upon myself almost wholly to transact that it kept me many hours awake in ye night. Y^e consiquence is I am late this morning. Ned sent before I was up to enquire after me & to know when I w^d have his Coach. I have now sent for it.

After I had sent away my Letter yesterday Ned call'd

me into his room & gave way to an Emotion of Grief that seem'd to releave him & which he had suppress'd out of attention to the poor afflicted Bro. & Sister. He told me that as Lady M. had left no orders or hinted her wish about her funeral, he sh^d beg of me to order it as I thought most respectful & proper. Her Will was open'd the day she dyed. She leaves £10,000 to her Sister £5000 to her Bro. £2000 to each of my Bro.'s younger children, £500 to Mrs Oliver, ditto to Nelly and to Mrs Heywood's daughters, to several of her god-children etc. To Lady Howe & her daughters, myself & many others to whom she meant only a token of regard £100 each. To Lord Middleton ye furniture of Middleton with some family Jewells & Plate, with other Legacies to friends & serv^{ts} amounting my Bro. thinks to about £50,000. The rest all to him.[1] My Bro. means to Bury her at Shipley. Indeed poor Mrs Whetham yesterday after sitting in silent sorrow for 2 hours said 'I hope Mr M. you mean to lay her where You hope to Lye yourself' & then bore Testimony to her having been ye happiest woman since her union with him that ever lived; it was she added too much for this World. My brother's attention to her & Chadwick & theirs to him gives me great pleasure. We have consulted them as far as their grief will allow us about every thing, but I hope I shall have an Able Counsellor to-day. Mrs Whetham express'd a wish to see Lady Howe in ye Letter Lyons wrote to her. If she comes she will take a weight from my Shoulders, because I shall be sure they will approve all she advises. But as to ye funeral it

---

[1] This was not quite the case, the child inheriting the bulk of its mother's large fortune, as mentioned later.

was necessary to determine it & being entirely my Bro.'s affair (tho' I think in general ye more private ye better) yet in her situation it appear'd to me that every show of respect short of an ostentatious parade was proper. I have therefore order'd 3 mourning coaches & my Bro.'s own Carriage containing all the upper servants to attend —Escutcheons etc. It is to set out on Monday get to Derby on friday night & be interr'd on Saturday; 8 Derbyshire gentlemen to be ask'd to bear ye Paul. . . .

Piccadilly 3 *o'Clock*.—I have had your kind Letter my dear Soul which is a true picture of your own Good Heart. Ned thanks you kindly but seems to think it will be best for ye three to remain together till ye whole of this Melancholy Business is over. I dissuade them from remaining here. If Ned cannot go far from Town he had better accept ye offer he has had of Ld Howe's house at Porters for a few days, then let Mrs Whetham & Chadwick go down to Kirklington & return just to transmit ye necessary business, of which he seems to think he has much that cannot wait. I don't believe he is any Judge of that at present, but perhaps a day or 2 will settle many things. No Letters from Lady Howe or from Harling[1] so we expect somebody is coming from both families. . .

Wednesday night 11 *o'Clock*.—We have settled much disagreable business to-day, but have a good deal still to come. . I was forc'd to call in my Bro. who went through it well, but he has been sadly low this afternoon & poor Mrs W. & Chadwick much worse than they were yesterday. Indeed I never saw poor Creatures so broken-hearted;

---

[1] Her sister Mrs. Barton's home in Norfolk.

she goes & weeps over ye Child 3 or 4 times a day in a most affecting manner.

Lady M. has left her her Pearl Bracelets & most of her Rings & Trinkets, so I advis'd my Bro. to give them to her directly to avoid renewal of grief. She took them, seal'd them up without looking at them & said she sh'd keep them for the Child. . . .

My Bro. shew'd me Lady M.'s Will written with her own hand & sign'd but not witness'd. She leaves £44,000 per ann. in annuities. Her fine Necklace & Earrings all ye Gilt & old Sideboard plate, Dressing Plate, Furniture of Middleton, China, Medals etc. to whoever shall be in possession of ye Title at her Death & to go with ye Title as long as it remains in ye Willoughby family. When all this is paid there will be including ye house more than £100,000 remaining. But nothing can lessen his loss of such a Woman. I came home intending to go to bed & now I am scribbling till 12 o'Clock.

9 *o'Clock Thursday 2nd July* 1789.—I slept better than I have done a long while, waked at 8 & got up. Shall write notes to Tradespeople to bring their goods to Chesterfield Street. I think I have little more to do now than to equip myself and Fanny [Mundy] If you have any Wants let me know or any message to Taylors etc. Don't you want Black Paper? . . . It is very irksome to me to be from you at this time particularly. It is a kind act your sending me & is as kindly taken & I am sure Ned will not wish to delay me when he feels he can go alone. I really do not know what he w^d have done without me. . . . Lord Howe is Ill so Lady H. can't come.

Thursday afternoon.—They are all three much better to-day than yesterday & we have talk'd over all this Melancholy business very Calmly. I urged them to fix some plan for themselves & again repeated your kind request that Ned w^d return with me. That I believe is really not practicable as he can do nothing until he has taken out Administration. In short my Dear Soul your kindness is ye Rock that supports us all & all our present distress'd Connections. I found they did not like to separate & therefore ventur'd to say I could Answer that you w^d gladly receive them all till they c^d fix their own plans, & was surpris'd to find no objection made to it from either. On the contrary it seems to be ye thing that suits best with their present feelings & your kind proposal of ye same Plan to-day (for it is now friday Noon) make all easy & delightful to me, though I have hardly a Nerve to tell you anything for we have just had a dismal interview with my two dear Sisters. They arrived at 12 last night. I was just steping into ye Coach to go home when Saml stop'd at the door & said they w^d be here in an hour. I returned to tell the News, but thought it better that they should not meet at that late hour, so sent them all to Bed & drove to Chesterfield Street. Y^e Meeting I need not describe. Nelly bore it better than Milly [Mrs. Barton] but both look dreadfully indeed. Barton came with them & I think will be of use to us in our Melancholy preparations for Tuesday. I stay'd with them an hour last night & then drove home, where my late return had put them in a fright.

This morn^g I had people of business upon appointment whom I was forced to dispatch before I c^d stir, but got some breakfast & set out at 11; walk'd through the Park which revived me, call'd in Piccadilly, found them very Low with ye Idea of seeing my Sisters. So I thought the sooner it was over ye better; order'd Ned's Coach to Chesterfield Street & set out to prepare them for it. Mrs. Whetham & Chadwick really behaved ye best of ye set. It has really been a trying affair. I fetch'd ye Babe down also that ye whole might be over at once. We have all wept over it till I can hardly see. I am going now to more tradespeople appointed to Chesterfield Street. My sisters are also going home. I shall return at 4 as Ned has just ask'd me not to leave Mrs. Whetham to-day & my Sisters will come again to Tea. I have not had a moment's talk with Nelly so know nothing of their intentions, but could I get ye Man [Mr. Barton] out of the way I w^d foster them also under your Wing, but I doubt that can't be. Hope I shall get back to you on Tuesday night. Ned etc. think they shall follow me on Saturday. . . .

Thank God for ye Charming Accts of to-day, that you are well & approve what I do is a cordial that will support me through anything. Indeed I am perfectly well but in a throng of melancholy business that tears my Heart to pieces all day long. Dear Ned is wonderfully calm, so are ye other two & they are upon a footing of mutual Confidence & openness that is a Comfort to themselves & very pleasing to see. . . . This day (Saturday) is the toping up of all orders & directions consequently a very busy working one for Body & Mind. . . . I told you they were all to remove to Porters to-morrow which I doubt by your Letter you do not quite approve. If it had been more respectful etc, I wish they had not moved till after Tuesday, which is ye day ye funeral is to set out. But it w^d have been a dreadful scene for them & you have named my taking Ned to sleep ye night before in Spring Gardens. People's own feelings must guide on all these occasions. Perhaps you will not approve of my setting out on Tuesday as the day is altered to that, but as I go from a different part of ye Town & sh'd set out many hours before ye funeral, My impatience to get to you made me see no impropriety in it. A like motive also made me press Ned to come to town to do business on Wednesday, but his own feelings has suggested that it will be improper for him to appear till after she is interr'd. So it is fixt that he shall not return here till Monday sennight & upon recollection that ye Body rests at Dunstable on Tuesday night & turns out of our Road from that Place, I shall effectually avoid it by not setting out till 7 or 8 o'Clock on Wednesday; but then I shall be late at Arbury. The passing it w^d be very Irksome to me & I sh'd think more exceptionable than preceding it by some hours. But if you are of a different opinion or in short if you disapprove of my setting out on Tuesday send a Letter off immediately. If it is too Late for the Mail it may be sent by ye Stage. Otherwise I shall try to drink Tea with you on Tuesday.

The House is freehold & ye Child's fortune which is £81,500 comes to ye father if she dyes an infant, but it is hers from ye death of ye mother. He cannot touch the income, therefore we must reckon the £700 annuitys to be deducted out of y^e £96,000 which is ye remainder after all Legacies are paid,—a noble Addition to his own fortune, but so far short of ye Income they Joyntly had, that a Change of Menage will be necessary. But these are after considerations, perhaps reserved for Arbury. He has offer'd Mrs. Whetham the Care of ye Child, at least for some time. Indeed the Consideration that her imence fortune w^d come to him in case of her Death w^d make it an too anxious charge for himself or Nelly. . . . Adieu.

4 *o'Clock*.—Lady Howe is just arrived. We were all together, a dismal meeting. I thought it better to come & dine with my sisters & go to them again at 7. . . .

We have glimpses of the progress of the motherless babe, 'the dear little Inocent Cause of all this misery,' in subsequent letters. She was christened Georgiana Elizabeth, and grew up, as far as we know, under the care of her aunt, Mrs. Whetham. A year later than the date of this last letter she was brought to London to be inoculated. In September 1791, when she would be more than two years old, Lady Newdigate was on a visit to her guardians, Mr. Chadwick and Mrs. Whetham, at Kirklington, and writes to Sir Roger concerning her:

The dear little Georgiana is ye fatest Little Pig you ever saw, perfectly Healthy & Lively & with ye same sweet intelligent Countenance, but her features are absolutely buried, so that she is not in my opinion so beautiful as when you saw her, but I dare not say that to Mrs. W. She never crys & will go to anybody; but her father & her nurse seem to divide her heart. Fanny also [her half-sister] has some share whilst she plays Country Dances to her, which she never fails to ask for in very expressive Language as soon as she is brought in after Dinner. . . .

The little heiress seems to have flourished in the atmosphere of love by which she was surrounded.

As soon as she was grown up, when just eighteen, Georgiana Mundy married Henry Pelham, fourth Duke of Newcastle. She became the mother of fourteen children, and died when only thirty-three, at the birth of twins, on September 27, 1822.[1]

[1] See *Debrett's Peerage*, Edition 1839.

CHAPTER VII

1790-1794

> The elder lady ... is tall, and looks the taller because her powdered hair is turned backward over a toupee, and surmounted by lace and ribbons. She is nearly fifty, but her complexion is still fresh and beautiful, with the beauty of an auburn blond; her proud pouting lips, and her head thrown a little backward as she walks, give an expression of hauteur which is not contradicted by the cold gray eye. The tucked-in kerchief rising full over the low tight bodice of her blue dress sets off the majestic form of her bust, and she treads the lawn as if she were one of Sir Joshua Reynolds's stately ladies who had suddenly stepped from her frame to enjoy the evening cool.—MR. GILFIL'S LOVE-STORY.

IN 1790 Lady Newdigate went up to London without Sir Roger, for the purpose of sitting to Romney for her full-length portrait, which now hangs in the saloon at Arbury, side by side with that of her husband by the same artist. She begins her journal-like letters to him as usual on the road, but it is not until she is in London that she describes her perplexing reception at Dunstable by Mrs. Oliver, the landlady, as follows:

I did not tell you last night how Mrs Oliver surpris'd me at Dunstable. She follow'd me & scrutiniz'd me in a Manner that made me think her either Drunk or Mad. At last she ask'd after you & on my answer that you was well she clap'd her hands together & exclaimed 'I am heartily glad to hear it; it has been reported that Sir Roger was shot dead by a highwayman.' The report has prevail'd some days in town, that it happen'd upon Uxbridge Common. Ned fortunately heard that circum-

stance which he knew must be false. He supposes that it arose from a Robbery that was committed there & a Jumble of yᵉ Story of Sir George Ramsay. . . .

Saturday 24*th April. Spring Gardens.*—Thank God that you are well . . . but I can't get that nasty story out of my Head. I charge you to throw out your Purse to any Man that Asks you for it as you come up & don't give him any pretence to shoot you. I shall take care & not walk yᵉ Streets that you may not find me dead or under yᵉ Surgeon's hands. The Stories in yᵉ papers of this horrid Woman Hater are not exaggerated. Not a night passes that some poor female is not dreadfully wounded. On Thursday evening Lady Howe's own Woman was assaulted at their own Door in Grafton Street. She saw this Monster following her & she ran forward & had time to ring yᵉ bell before he came up, but yᵉ porter not being in yᵉ Hall, the Man threw her down upon yᵉ Steps, kick'd & punch'd her till she fainted away & then stab'd her in yᵉ thigh. In this Condition she was found when yᵉ Door was open'd. Ned yesterday saw a young Lady who was only slightly wounded by means of yᵉ Man missing his Stroke which was aim'd at her hip. The Knife or Dagger whatever it is went through a thick bundle of muslins which she had in her pocket & cut a gash in her thigh. A premium of 100 Guineas is offer'd & subscrib'd yet nobody can lay hold of him.

I am settled as if I had been here a month, but your Rooms below & above look so Melancholy and *wanting*, I can't bear them. I find my Brother's carriage has so much Employment with himself his daughter [Fanny] Nelly & Milly [Miss Mundy and Mrs. Barton] that I think

I shall feel more at my Ease to have a Carriage than a Chair. Nelly offers me her Chariot & last night I accepted it, but have just had Newport [the carriage builder] with me who offers me a good Chariot for a guinea which I had rather give than feel in pain for what belongs to another. . . . The Pics [Mundys in Piccadilly] seem all very well, but Ned's spirits are so entirely gone, that he makes my heart ach. . . . Love to Sally, adieu.

11 *o'Clock Monday.*—Nelly & Ned have beat me out of my Apothecaries Chariot; to be sure it was a beastly thing that Mr Newport sent me, so I have now got Nelly's with my own Harness & Coat. I am vastly well & Mr Barton [Milly's husband] who came to town last night complim^{ts} my looks greatly, so I hope Mr Romney will like me to-morrow. They are all mightily dissatisfy'd with my Picture, but as you think you shall like it they shall not make him do it again, unless Lady Templetown & Romney himself wish it. I will call & take Lady T. with me. Fanny [Mundy] coughs & looks sadly, Ned is so allarm'd that he has sent privately to desire Sir Lucas Peppys will call & say whether she ought not to be sent into ye Country. . . . I am glad your little Companion amuses you. I have bought her ye Music of ye Haunted Tower which Fanny plays all day long, but wants Sally to sing ye Songs which are very pretty. Adieu, adieu.

Wednesday morn^g 28th April 1790.—. . . Lady Templetown was not at home yesterday. I left word I sh'd be found at Romney's till four & beg'd to see her, but she never came. My picture is still too young & too handsome, but I fancy you will like it. . . . I am going with Ned to-day who is sitting . . . to Lawrence. If I like him he shall sit for me. . . . Romney thinks he shall be satisfy'd with one sitting from you, but tells me I must supply your place on Tuesday. . . . I have just bought & sent to Wolter to bind a Book to tear Sally's brain & my own to pieces. I have paid no Money yet except for Music. Apropos to y^c head I sh'd be glad if you c^d bring me when you come my White Beaver Hat. . . . I can forgive if you sh'd forget this Commission but not if you neglect to send me a handsome smooth Lock of y^r own hair. What I have was taken from ye Toopee & is of all lengths. What was cut off when you left off your queue w^d be just the thing. Let it come in your next Letter. . . . A great knock at ye Door. Enter Lady Templetown & Ld Feilding. They have stay'd till I was obliged to turn them out & now I must dress & whirl away to Pic.

Saturday morning.—. . . A note from Romney to desire me to dress myself in white Sattin before I come to him to-day; I have no such thing in town, must get my head dress'd in haste & drive to Pic & borrow a Gown which I shall not be able to get into. . . . Time to go to Romney.

4 o'Clock.—Lady T. was faithless & never came to me, but my sisters approve ye figure & attitude which was ye business to-day. The Borrow'd Gown won't satisfy him, he insists upon my having a rich white Sattin with a long train made by Tuesday & to have it left with him all summer. It is ye oddest thing I ever knew, but I dare not disobey him as you are not here to support me. I had just read a Charming Letter from you & a very good one indeed from Sally or I think he w^d have put me out of humour. . . .

Monday.—I met Motta at ye Door in Pic, & Nelly ask'd him to dine there to-day. I have not seen him except at ye Opera, he has been at Portsmouth with ye King of Spain's Physicians. . . . I have got a white Gown for Mr. Romney to-morrow. Adieu.

Romney's portrait of Lady Newdigate was a long time on hand. She was still sitting to him in London two years later.

The Lady Templetown, on whose artistic taste and judgment Sir Roger placed so much dependence, was a Miss Boughton by birth, and at this time the widow of the first Baron Templetown. Her son afterwards became the first viscount of that name. She was an old friend and correspondent of Sir Roger's—'Your Baroness,' as Lady Newdigate often calls her in her letters to her husband.

At the later period mentioned above—1792—Lady Newdigate gives Sir Roger an account of one of her final sittings to Romney.

I finish'd yesterday in an anxious minute. You will not disapprove that I w^d not let Romney fix all that Care upon my Brow. . . . I am appointed by Romney at 12 o'Clock. Lady Templetown and Mrs C. Cotton are to meet me. If the former dislikes my Countenance he shall do nothing to y^r face for y^e last Sitting was thought to improve me.

4 o'Clock.—Romney kept me 2 hours and $\frac{1}{2}$. Lady T. was there almost y^e whole time. I read to them your directions which they seem perfectly to Comprehend & approve. Romney cannot part with y^e drawings till y^e pictures are quite finish'd, but promises to take care of them. I fancy I call'd up very good looks to-day; where they came from I don't know, but my Picture is certainly much improv'd. All seem satisfy'd with it. I have reason to be so, for it is handsomer than ever I was in my life.

Lady Templetown gives her verdict on Lady Newdigate's portrait in a letter to Sir Roger, dated

Portland Place: June 11th 1792.

The unanswered letter of a Friend is a silent reproach that I had rather not feel, & it seems an injury to myself to appear negligent where I am very sincerely attached at all times and interested to preserve the favorable ground I stood upon. At the time my good Sir that I received your Letter I was engaged in very sad duties, & the course of the winter has been with me *so unquiet* that I should be sorry to be called to a strict account of all my omissions altho' *la cara moglie* will have told you that I did not neglect the task you imposed upon me relative to my *then* neighbour Mr Romney, & I really think he has acquitted himself well in respect to Lady Newdigate. The character of the face is well preserved, & the hair is of an agreable *duskiness* that is neither in nor out of powder, so that I am of opinion it will please all parties—not that I am willing to make this compromise in order to give up our little *skirmishes* upon the subject, & which I shall rejoice in any opportunity of repeating.

We were *not guilty* of passing by Arbury *unheeded* last year, for I did not go to Ireland. If I live till this time twelvemonth I probably shall, but one trembles in forming any distant plans, however ardently we may wish that no sad circumstance may interrupt their accomplishment.

I understand that you are soon to have the pleasure of seeing Mrs Nelly Mundy & her charming niece [Fanny Mundy] at Arbury—charming indeed I think her & one of the most pleasing young women in London. I am now preparing with great expedition to set out for Sysa, but as you may suppose I shall not travel through France, & have no apprehension of being molested in any part of Austrian Flanders. I take my 3 Nymphs with me & conduct Arthur so far on his way to a College at Marbourg where he is to acquire the french & german languages, so essential to a soldier,—the rest of my flock are *tolerably sound both in mind and body—c'est tout ce qu'on peut espérer.*

My kindest Compliments I beg to L^dy Newdigate. Templetown would entreat me to present his best respects if he was near me. Eliza is sea-bathing at Ramsgate wth little Sophia & Caroline remains to console me at home. This is a domestic Chronicle & I will conclude it with the truest assurance of my being ever my dear Sir

Y^r affec^ate & faithful Servant

E. TEMPLETOWN.

Romney seems to have lingered for another year or two over the completion of his two portraits of Sir Roger and Lady Newdigate. We do not hear of their being sent down to Arbury until 1794, when the saloon, with its Gothic ceiling adapted from Henry VII.'s Chapel at Westminster, was ready to receive them. Whilst these prolonged artistic sittings were going on, entailing frequent visits to London, Sally's musical education was by no means neglected. Signor Motta continued to be her capable and appreciative master, both at Arbury and in London, until he was taken ill at the former place and died in October 1791. His premature loss was a subject of much regret, both to the Newdigate and Mundy families, who evidently valued him as a friend as well as a musician. Motta's death at Arbury caused no little trouble to Sir Roger, who was a long time searching for the deceased man's rightful heirs, to whom he could consign such property as he had left behind him. His body was laid in the grave at the parish church of Chilvers Coton, and a tablet to his memory was placed in the church [1] by Sir Roger.

Lady Templetown, having gone to Italy for a prolonged stay, as anticipated in her letter given above, was able to be of use to Sir Roger in his efforts to discover Motta's relations. She writes from Portice, 20th September, 1794:

The receiving a letter from my good friend Sir Roger Newdigate was an unexpected & very sincere pleasure to me and I cannot delay the reply until the objects are attained that he wishes for. Perhaps Sir William Hamilton may already have acquainted you with the steps he had taken, at any rate it may be satisfactory to you to know that as far as it depends on me I will hasten the conclusion of the business, but Sir W^m having been for some time at Castelamare & myself always at Portice prevents my seeing even his Secretary who has had directions from Sir William to get Motta's Brothers from Calabria without loss of time & procure a legal power to enable Mr. Manby to transmit to them his effects, which being done his Secretary was to give me immediate information. But Sir W^m said this might take up three weeks at least but (entre nous) I was pleased to see that he seemed to enter earnestly into the business—for he latterly appears to throw aside all cares but for his *capital Gem* & his Etruscan Vases, of which he has certainly a most magnificent

---

[1] 'Sacred to the memory of Domenic Motta, of the Kingdom of Naples, who died at Arbury, October 31, 1791.'

collection. .... However to return to poor Motta which is at this time more interesting as a Capital of £300 would relieve his Relations from indigence & perhaps enable them to enter into some means of trade, by which numbers in Calabria have made comfortable fortunes. Sir W^m says that neither the Prince Castel Cicala nor his Secretary would make any scruple of pocketing the money if it once got into their hands as they are absolutely necessitous and the Secretary a kind of Attorney.

I had great pleasure in seeing M^r and Mrs Newdigate at Naples where I wish'd to seduce them to stay a little longer, but he always repeated a sentence of yours in one of your letters, *that if they did they would repent it*. .... It was my fixed intention to have set out about this time on my way to England had not these scourges of Mankind made such an undertaking absolutely hazardous & I believe impracticable. I had rather be destroyed by the burning Monster that is near us, than by those new species of Barbarians. But heaven's will must be accomplished by different means & we must endeavour always to think that ' there is some soul of goodness in things evil, would men observingly distil it out.'

I would fain have heard a great deal more of Arbury and of dear Lady Newdigate to whom I desire to be affectionately remembered. My Girls are very much obliged by your remembrance of them. I should like to shew them to you, for as girls go they are not amiss. . . .

I have never heard whether my favourite Miss Mundy is married or not—if the Men had any taste she certainly would—altho' perhaps she might not improve by the change. I often think that was I sure of living & *seeing* fifteen years longer I should not be in a hurry to marry my girls. Are you of my opinion?[1] . . .

There is a letter of the same year written from Naples by Mrs. Francis Newdigate to Sir Roger, giving an account of a day spent in company with Sir William Hamilton and his wife. As the latter has been rendered memorable by Romney's art and Nelson's love, it may be interesting to give a contemporaneous estimate of this lady.

Mrs. Newdigate writes on the 18th of May, 1794:

MY DEAR SIR,—Sir W^m & Lady Hamilton came to visit us the day after we sent them our good Col's [Hamilton's] letter & fixed last Sunday for our spending the day with them at Caserta, which we did and I think in the whole course of my Life I never was so much amused. Sir W^m received us in the most friendly manner &' his Wife did all she possibly c^d to be agreable & succeeded so well that at 8 o'Clock in the Even^g we were excessively sorry to go. We arrived there at 10 in the morn^g & found Sir W^m & Lady H. playing & singing with several musicians. Lady H. sang several songs most inchantingly & made us all very sorry to go & see the aqueduct & the Palace. They attended us & we came back at three o'Clock to dinner. The moment it was over they took us to see the King's beautifull English garden which Sir W^m has had the direction of intirely. Nothing can be imagined more beautifull, the turf he has contrived to throw water over whenever he pleases, the verdure is astonishing, the finest exoticks grow like common shrubs. We were no sooner in the midst of the garden than the Queen & all her

---

[1] Lady Templetown's eldest daughter, Elizabeth, married the first Marquess of Bristol; the second, Caroline, became Mrs. Singleton; and the youngest, Sophia, remained unmarried.

family arrived & insisted on our being presented to her at that time. She talked a great deal very graciously to us. As I knew she made it a rule to meet all the English that the Hamiltons take into the garden we had taken the precaution of being rather more dress'd than usual. I was quite in Love with Sir W^m & much charmed with my Lady who appears to me quite a pattern of good conduct. She is grown amazingly large but is still very handsome. She sang us some beautiful little Pollish songs & promised Mr. Newdigate to give him leave to get them coppied, tho' she never had given them away to anybody. . . . They have made us promise to spend another day with them next week when they come to Naples. . . .

CHAPTER VIII

1792

> While Cheverel Manor was growing from ugliness into beauty, Caterina, too, was growing from a little yellow bantling into a whiter maiden, with no positive beauty indeed, but with a certain light, airy grace which, with her large appealing dark eyes, and a voice that, in its low-toned tenderness, recalled the love-notes of the stock-dove, gave her a more than usual charm.—MR. GILFIL'S LOVE-STORY.

WE must retrace our steps a couple of years, from the date of the last letter to the spring of 1792, when Lady Newdigate came up to London to assist at the presentation at Court of her niece, Fanny Mundy. This was the girl of whom Lady Templetown wrote as 'that charming Miss Mundy,' 'one of the most pleasing young women in London,' &c.

Sally Shilton, now seventeen or eighteen years old, was also brought to London this spring, to test her powers as a songstress, more especially with a view to her training for a professional career. In Lady Newdigate's letters to Sir Roger she frequently mentions her desire to be guided in this matter by the advice of a Mr. and Mrs. Bates. The former was Joah Bates, an eminent musician, born at Halifax in Yorkshire in 1740. He was unanimously chosen conductor of the commemoration of Handel at Westminster Abbey; and till the year 1793 he conducted the choral performances of ancient music. His wife was a first-rate singer.[1]

Lady Newdigate's first letter given here is from Dunstable, her usual stopping place on the road to London. This time she was to take up her abode with her brother in Piccadilly, Sir Roger's own house in Spring Gardens being for sale.

---

[1] Maunder's *Biographical Treasury*, 1845.

Dunstable, Wednesday 9 *o'Clock. Feb^{ry}* 1792.—Sally's head got well after we had devour'd 3 pounds of Cold Beef & she has been reading y^e Marquis de Boselle to me from y^e time we arrived which was at $\frac{1}{2}$ past till 6 y^e time a dish of fine plump larks were set upon y^e table . . . & now she is almost asleep over y^e fire. . . . Had we resolved to stop at Stoney Stratford not a Bed was there for us at y^e Cock. Lady Uxbridge had order'd a Dinner to be ready at 5 & Engag'd every Bed in y^e house & when we stop'd at this Door Mrs. Oliver told me with a Melancholy face that she had already 3 Families in ye house & had nothing but Garrets to offer me. I did not like the thoughts of going to a strange house so determined to wait till she c^d see what she c^d procure for me, & she very soon conducted me in a good Dining Room & shew'd me a neat 2 bed Garret where I dare say we shall sleep as well as in a Palace. . . .

Friday evening Piccadilly.—. . . Thursday next will be a hurrying day for it is fixt for ye presentation & after much pro & Co. it is determined that Nelly [Mundy] goes also. I am very glad, it makes Ned happy & will put both Aunt & Niece upon a more respectable footing & be vastly pleasanter to me. We have been to various shops to see fashions, . . . but to-morrow is to determine ye weighty points of Dress. Sally has been out with us and has had a present of a Cap & a Bonnet. Nelly & Fanny think she looks thin & is Grave but I hope it is only with silent wonder at ye New Scene. They are all very kind & good to her. . . . Ld Feilding Din'd & stay'd all ye evening yesterday & both ye Girls sung a great deal, but I do not think Sally's Voice sounds so strong as it

did at Arbury. I hope it is only ye difference of ye room.
... I sent to the Bates to say we shall be glad if they
will call upon us & that we will call upon them in a day
or two. I talk'd to Miss Colmore about a Master for
Sally ... the whole family are to drink tea with us this
evening when we shall discuss ye subject fully. ... Sad
acc^t of ye P. of W. & Duke of Y. They are beastly drunk
every day & People say ye poor little Duchess is very unhappy. It is supposed she will open her house & let in all
ye world on Thursday next; we shall probably make part
of ye Crowd. I say *we* for you may expect I shall be very
dissipated when we once set off. ...

Sunday.—Colmores sent an Excuse last night but
they come to us this evening. I doubt Sally won't be
able to sing to them for she had ye head ach all day.

Monday 4 *o'Clock.*—Sally Rally'd last night and sung
Charmingly to ye Colmores; they were all much pleas'd
& Miss C. thinks her Voice is grown stronger. Mrs. C.
ask'd us to Dine with them on friday & enquired if I sh'd
have any Objection to let Sally come to them at 7 as she
possibly might have a few Musical people. It is Just y^e
thing I wish & better for her that she is not ask'd to
Dinner. ... We were deny'd at ye Bates but I left a
note to say I wish'd to see them either at their own house
or here, & desired they would let me know. They tell me
it is said to be in agitation for Mrs. B. to come out again
as a publick singer. How will that operate in regard to
our business? Miss Colmore promised to go to Lady
Clarges this morning to ask her opinion about the 1st
Master. ...

Tuesday.—This day has been all Hurry which indeed

our Mornings have hitherto been, & we are as quiet in ye Evenings. Few People know we are in town, & we have not yet set out of an Evening, not do not intend it till thursday.

I have call'd upon & found Lady Templetown & agreed that we'll do all that you shall command but must wait till our great Hurrys are over. It quite turns my head to think of Thursday; sale of the house, Court and God knows what by that time may happen. I think I am in a Charming Train about Sally. I gave her a dose of Evans yesterday & she seems quite well to-day. She is at this instant under a french hair Dresser's hands to be Cut & Curl'd, but not Powder'd I promise you, & I am going to take off her Stays which will also please you. I agree to ye proposal of ye Colmores for Sunday & have hopes we shall gain credit & make friends. By Miss C.'s note I rather think Music is given up for Friday. I have desired that may be explain'd because in that Case Sally shall not go. I have not an Answer from ye Bates. Nelly and I are going to ye City and shall pass near, so if time will serve we'll call again.

You may suppose we are very busy Equipping ourselves, everything is fixt upon, & Sally shall write an account of us when we are Compleat. 4 *o'Clock*—Just return'd from ye City, call'd again in John Street. Bates's are in Norfolk & the Maid does not know when they come back—very unlucky, but we find an invitation from Mrs. Gally to Music on Monday to meet ye Anguishes. Perhaps I may hear from them when they come. . . .

Wednesday night.—I have just had ye enclosed from Miss Colmore, so ye Music party stands for Friday & I cannot wait upon yᵉ Marchˢˢ [of Donegall] which I am sorry for. She has call'd both mornᵍ & Evening & left Tickets [cards] also for my Sister & Niece. I have also been twice at her Door. What an impertinent Fine Lady is Lady Clarges! I wᵈ not condescend to be disappointed in my Answer to Miss Colmore as to having Pozzi to accompany Sally. I left that to Miss C.'s judgment telling her that I had determined to have Mortellari to teach her. Every one agrees that he is yᵉ best & has the Name. . . . Fanny is also to learn of him.

I went for an hour to Lady Dacre last night; found her with only Mrs. Munster & Miss Lennard. She recᵈ me most kindly & ask'd a thousand questions about you & Arbury. We all Join'd in Abusing you for not coming up with me. By the by Lᵈʸ D. seem'd very sure that Bates wᵈ be at yᵉ Antient Music to-night & promised if she saw him to tell him that I wanted much to see him. Mrs. Bates has been Ill & out of town 3 weeks & Bates has been with her, but he is Manager of yᵉ Ant. Music & therefore cannot well be absent. When I came home at 10 o'Clock I found Lady Templetown. She had invited herself to Sup & stay till her Son Lᵈ T. call'd for her after yᵉ Opera. Ned return'd from yᵉ Opera just as we sat down to Table, said yᵉ Opera was stupid & yᵉ house cold & empty. It was near 12 when Lᵈ T. arrived very hungry & in raptures with everything he had heard & seen. This disagreement of opinion cannot be owing entirely to yᵉ difference between yᵉ Age of 20 & 40.

Thursday mornᵍ 9 o'Clock.—I have slept well & feel equal to yᵉ importance of yᵉ day. The Court affair will be made very easy to us. Lady Harcourt is very obliging &

will explain to the Queen the affair of Nelly; & Lady Bath is in Waiting with whom she is acquainted. Gowns are promised in time & all things Else are ready. You have added greatly to ye Beauty of Fanny's Dress. I thought I could not execute your kind intentions towards her at a better time nor in a better way than by getting her a Gold Chain for her Neck to hang her father's picture to. It is quite *the thing* & will cost you about 4 guineas & ½. I have not time nor Room for ye Joy & thanks she expresses. My Hair dresser comes at ½ past 10 so hope I shall have no hurry. I have got a new Hat for John as you said I might & I believe ye Chair & Chair Men will look Clean & Tidy.

Maberley [the family solicitor] has been here . . . & will attend the sale [of the house] & meet me here when I come from Court which will be time enough to add a postscript to you. There will be no York House to-morrow. We are all glad of it. All hurry, hurry, Bellman ringing. . . .

½ *past* 4 *o'Clock*.—All our Court business is happily over & we have got off our Hoops & are Comfortable tho' I am still ignorant of my fortune, for Maberley is not arriv'd so in ye meantime I will tell you we were graciously received. Lady Harcourt behaved very politely, came & stood by Nelly when ye Queen came up, & everything pass'd well & Fanny Look'd so. She was a very Eligant figure & we are all so well pleas'd & so little fatigued that we have accepted ye offer of Mrs. Barwell's Box at ye Play to-night & Sally is of ye Party. I must tell you that Lady Donegal—but here enters Mr Maberley. The house is purchased by Mr Bumell of the Treasury, late under Secretary to Ld North. There were no bidders but himself beyond 2000 Guineas. Our Puff got him up to 2850 Guineas which is £2992, 10. Therefore had ye puff bid again the house Mr M. thinks w^d have been bought in, exceeding your Authority. I am perfectly satisfy'd & hope you are so. . . .

Saturday morning 16*th Feb*^{ry} 1792.—We have not any of us suffer'd in ye least from ye Business & hurry of thursday, tho' ye day was piercing cold, a proof that we are all well & stout. . . . We are all delighted with ye new Opera House (if it is not too large to hear well) & the procession of Simon is magnificent. Mrs Barwell's Box is well placed for hearing & seeing; she has ye goodness to lend it us again for to-night when Mrs. Siddons acts Lady Macbeth & Mrs. Jordan is in ye Farce. So you see we make all possible use of our time. I shall take Sally again. She did herself great credit last night but there were few *Worthy People* to hear her, the great Judges all disappointed Mrs. Colmore, but all present were delighted & will spread her fame & Lady Clarges has been with Miss C. to ask if she c^d not bring Sally to meet Mortellari at her house on Monday evening. I am quite glad, so is Miss Colmore, also that she is really engaged to sing with the Anguishes at Mrs. Gally's. I have sent through Miss Colmore to engage Mortellari to come & teach both Fanny & Sally. The Latter shall have a Lesson every day if he can give it, & Sally is now gone to Chuse & hire herself a piano forte at Broadrip's which I shall set in ye dressing Room which Nelly gives up to me, so she may have her full practice without encroaching upon Fanny. I hope you will think we are in good train. The only fear I have is of her strength. She looks very pale & peeking to-day

& tells me that she was wak'd in yᵉ night with yᵉ numbness in her head & face of which she has before complain'd but not lately. I have always thought it to be nervous & if so yʳ exertion of spirits & voice yesterday wᵈ occasion it. I will not let her sing at all to-day. Colmore's Dinner was ridiculously Magnificent, only our family & four men; 2 Emense Courses, full Desert with Ices, Champaign & in short every kind of fine Wine. We sat down to Table at 6 & did not rise till ½ past 8. I never was so tired, Sally was waiting in yᵉ Room above from 7 o'Clock, & we got home just at 12, ate our Crust & went to Bed, & Nelly desires I will tell you we have not had one Collogue after Eleven o'Clock since I came to town, can you credit such goodness? I assure you we are as prudent as we are Active; it is impossible for things to go on more pleasantly. If you really have no remains of Gout or Sickness (& I trust that you tell me yᵉ very truth) & go on pleasantly with your Companions I shall like to enjoy mine a Little after our hurrys are over. . . . Have ordered a Coachman's great Coat. . . . We can do without a Hat till after thursday when we must attend Sᵗ James's again & then one of my Chair Men's hats may be loop'd properly to serve. . . . I forgot to say that Colmore has seen Molini who inform'd him that he had learnt at yᵉ Neapolitan Ministers that Motta's friends knew of his Death, so they conclude yᵉ same packet will have brought Letters for you. . . .

Sunday.—I have had another Vexation about your Box. Lady Templetown, Sir John Anstruther, Mrs. Cotton, etc. etc. kept me so long from Dressing for yᵉ Early Dinner as we were to see Mrs. Siddons that I pack'd in a hurry & left out your Snuff, which I hope you do not want, but it looks as if I had less attention to you than I ought to have. Pray do not think so, even if I fail in other instances for indeed my Mind is occupy'd with such variety of interesting subjects that I don't know how to govern it. . . . It has snowed so hard all morning that we have none of us Ventur'd to Church but y^r Brother & 2 Sisters have had a long Collogue, the first without interruptions since we met. . . . I believe he [Barton] dines here & Lord Feilding & we stay at home to Chuse & rehearse the Songs & Duetts that the Girls are to perform to-morrow.

Monday.—. . . Past 3½, I must dress & dine with the March^{ss} of Donegal[1] at 5. . . Y^r Noble Nephew is not in town & nothing ever was more obliging than L^{dy} Donegal has been to us all, called 3 times & left tickets [cards] for all; at Court when she heard we were come to present Fanny desired she might stand by us, so don't be sorry that I dine with her.

Tuesday.—How you w^d have been pleased to hear the applause our Little Syren gain'd last night at Mrs. Gally's where many Musical people & some of acknowledged taste & Judgment were assembled. None sang but ye 3 Miss Anguishes & herself; they were cut down by her most exceedingly. Miss Charlotte who is ye great singer sung ' vi diro ' in so infamous a Stile that we did not like ye Song at all. Everybody agrees that Sally will be a very Capital Singer when she comes to her full strength, but

---

[1] Sir Roger's nephew, Lord Donegall, had married for the third time in 1790, and was advanced in the Irish peerage to be Marquis of Donegall and Earl of Belfast in 1791.

that till that time she must be managed with attention or she may lose her Voice if not her life. This was ye general opinion last night & Miss Colmore who is quite Wild about her is very Ernest with me not to let Mortellari or any Professional People who may think to gain Money or Credit by her Exhibition prevail with me to let her be heard in a Publick Room these 2 years to come, by which time she will have acquired strength & Knowledge in Musick to command Applause. I shall suspend my decided opinion till I have heard that of Mr. Bates who I have as yet no Message from, but I do not see in what light I can send to consult Giardini. If I sh'd meet him at any Musical party wch I am afraid is not likely I c^d ask his opinion, but he has already given it to M^r. Payne who you know told us that Mr. Giardini said she w^d in 2 or 3 years be a fine singer, but that her Voice was not fit for ye Publick at present; & w^d it not be awkward to give him ye trouble of coming to Me here without making him any recompense or agreeing to his recommendation, which doubtless w^d be a person he wish'd to serve. I have employ'd Miss Colmore to engage Mortellari who is by All acknowledg'd to be ye 1st in taste & that is all that Sally can improve by, for she is better grounded than any of them; but if you still think I sh'd still send for Giardini tell me but ye manner how & I will do it. I send you another proof that her fame is gone abroad & I do think that to have her solicited in this manner will gain her many more friends & admirers than it w^d do to try her in any Publick Room. But all that may still be managed if it is thought Eligible. Be assured I will not be inattentive to her interest, you see she has a full share

SALLY SHILTON IN LONDON

of my thought. I take Fanny & Sally to-night into ye Pit to ye Opera. The Coach is now at ye Door to Carry me to Lady Donegal, Colmores etc. etc. Ld D. came home before Dinner yesterday & flirted with me so much that you w^d have been quite Jealous had you seen it. He bids me tell Sir Roger he w^d come to Arbury as soon as he gets to Fisherwick. . . . She is very pleasing indeed & I find we are to be very intimate. . . .

4 o'Clock.—We met Mortellari at ye Colmore's & Fanny sung a Duett with him; he is to come to her to-morrow at 3 & to Sally at seven. I like his manner much. . . .

Thursday.—. . . I am now dress'd for Court & to dine as I told you with the Marquis & March^ss. I hope you will no longer disapprove when I shall have time to tell you ye speeches he has made & his Civilities to my Brother & all of us. . . . I will tell Sally to fill up ye other half Sheet whilst I am at Court as I fear I shall not have time to add anything. I am wonderfully well & Sally also I assure you.

From Sally Shilton to Sir Roger

SIR,—I am happy to tell you that Lady Newdigate is in perfect health. She left me to add a Little to her Letter whilst she is at Court. M^rs [Nelly] & Miss Mundy [were] looking very well in their Court dresses, and the latter is in perfect health and quite fat. They are all going to dine at the Marquis of Donegal's and after that M^r & Miss Mundy go to Cumberland House—in short they are very dissipate. We went to the opera last Tuesday Evening, they make very bad work of it. I have got Mortellari for singing, I did not like him at First but like him very well now. Lady Newdigate is so good as to let him come four times a week to me; thank God I am in very good health at present and hope to continue so, and my voice is in very good order. Mortellari says that I know a great deal of Musick; he brought me some new songs which I sang off at sight, which is a great comfort. Lady Newdigate and I go next Tuesday Evening to Lady Dacre to have a little Musick and Lady N. thinks she will meet Mr. Bates there. We have expected him here a great wile, but he is so busy in his Custom house that he hardly finds time to eat his dinner. I believe Mrs. Bates is not in town. She is gone into the Country for her health. I am very happy to hear that you are so well.

I am your ever
Dutiful & Obed^t Servant
SARAH SHILTON.

From Lady Newdigate

½ *past* 4.—I think I have taken Leave of Royalty for ye rest of my Life, & a very handsome Leave they took of me. It was a very full drawing room, we are but this instant got home, but what will be that on Tuesday? All ye World will be presented (I excepted) to ye Dutchess of York. . . .

Thursday night ½ *past* 10.—We have had a chearful pleasant Dinner & stay'd till 9 o'Clock. His Lordship had so much to say to his Aunt & so many messages to send to his Uncle, that to say the truth she was thoroughly tired, but ye rest of the party consisting of ye March^ss [1] & Miss Godfrey, Nelly & Fanny, Lord Sackville, his Brother, my Bro. & Doct^r Morgan were so well amused with Conversation & the Irish Bag Pipe that they w^d not attend to my signs to come away. I had ye whole story of Ld Belfast & a sad one it is; he is indicted for Perjury & there is to be a big tryal before Ld Kenyon on Tuesday next. I c^d not make head or tail of ye Story from his Lordship except that the foolish young Man had been bamboozled out of £40,000 in ye space of nine months by some Villanous People who to cover their own Iniquity had commenced this suit against him, but L^{dy} D. says they have no doubt but he will be honorably acquitted. I am really sorry for the Father, he seems to feel much more than he knows how to express & desired me ten times over to write you ye whole story & to tell you that his Mind has been so occupy'd for some months past, that he has omitted doing what was right by you, but he will wait upon you at Arbury & will write to you himself when this important tryal is determined, & he hopes you will consent to my staying in town a Month Longer to be present when Ld B. returns from his banishment, as he thinks so near a relation as Sir Roger sh^d be present either in person or by deputy on that occasion. What a strange head! he will send me his 6 Tickets for Hastings's Tryal on Wednesday. We are all quite in Love with her. She appears every time we see her more pleasing, but enough of them. . . .

[1] This Lady Donegall was Barbara, daughter of the Rev. Doctor Luke Godfrey, and married Lord Donegall as his third wife in 1790.

CHAPTER IX

1792

> This rare gift of song endeared her (Caterina) to Lady Cheverel, who loved music above all things, and it associated her at once with the pleasures of the drawing-room. Insensibly she came to be regarded as one of the family, and the servants began to understand that Miss Sarti was to be a lady after all.—MR. GILFIL'S LOVE-STORY.

LADY NEWDIGATE had family anxieties at this time which she was sharing with her brother, Mr. Mundy, and her sister Nelly in regard to their sister Milly's husband— Mr. Barton. The latter had long been a trouble and an object of dislike to his wife's family, and now owing to gambling debts was on the verge of ruin. Sir Roger, with his customary warm-heartedness, was not only ready with his counsel in this difficulty, but was quite willing and anxious to receive Mrs. Barton at Arbury, if it could be of any assistance at the expected crisis. In after years Mrs. Barton seems to have been a constant visitor, if not a resident, at Arbury.

At the present moment Lady Newdigate's mind was also much harassed by perplexities in regard to her *protégée* Sally, and Sir Roger probably added to them by his peremptory and urgent desire for the girl's immediate *début* as a professional singer. Lady Newdigate combats this idea in her usual tactful way in the next letter from London, which is in continuation of the series begun in the last chapter.

Friday Piccadilly 3 *o'Clock.*— . . . Your determined opinion about Sally's being produced so opposite to that of others who I have consulted as unprejudiced Judges worrys me I must confess. But be assured that everything I have yet done is in favour of your plan, that I will talk to Bates in that stile & as far as I find it practicable it shall be adopted. All these Little exhibitions are to announce her to ye World as a professional singer. Mortellari teaches her as such & is giving her an Artful Manner of throwing out her Voice to be heard in publick. The fault he finds is that she sings *en Dame* & not *en professor*. I am sending her to-night to ye Oratorio to hear Harrison & Mrs. Billington in 'Sweet Bird' & many of her fine Handel songs, & on Saturday (to-morrow sennight) Nelly makes a Concert here in order to Collect all ye best Judges & every means is tried to induce ye Bates's to come to us that day & before, if it is possible to get them. I am sure if my own Bread depended on it I c^d do no more for her. Indeed I am more anxious for her Welfare than is consistent with my own Comfort, & I begin to suspect that she will in future give me pain instead of pleasure in reward for all the time & Care I have spent upon her. I do not mean to insinuate a Complaint against her, but such Dangers & difficulties appear in sending her out, & she must lose so much Countinance, protection & consequence whenever that happens. But no more on this subject until I have seen Bates. . . .

Saturday.—. . . Sally was delighted with the Oratorio last night. I sent Mrs. Rhodes & Mr. Lyons with her into ye Front Box. The Crowd was expected to be so great I durst not venture her into ye Pit or Gallery. Mortellari takes a vast deal of pains with her, & I think has taught her Art in putting out her Voice. I am going to take her to another Little Party at Mrs. Gally's to-night.

But Nelly forbids me to think & write so much about her; she says that except the time that the Spring Gar. House engages me all my thoughts & arrangements are given up to Sally; that ever since I came into this house we have never had one ½ hour's tete-a-tete Conversation, nor ever seen ye poor Clavicellos since ye 1st night we unpack'd them. All this is very true, for my mornings if I am not at Sp: Gar: are spent with business & papers at ye opposite Corner of the house from her, & between Fanny's introduction & ye parties we attend on Sally's acc^t we are too much fagg'd with ye day to Collogue at night. She bids me tell you she is quite Jealous of Sally & shall send her back to Arbury if I don't give a Little more of my attention to my Hostess. Indeed I ought for both Ned & all his house study my ease & pleasure & make my Situation very pleasant & Comfortable. Your Letter of 3 pages is just arrived, two of them entirely engross'd by Sally. Indeed we both make her too great an object. Give me leave to assure you my Dear Love, that there is not a single argument you have used that I have not thought on & duly weigh'd & that I will not by personal affection, self-interest or any Consideration for myself, You, or anything else be influenced from doing what appears to me to be for her Welfare both present & future—that I think it a duty to act for her to the best of my Judgment & will do so. . . .

Monday.—. . . As I heard nothing from Bates I yesterday wrote a long letter to Mrs. B. explaining my Motive for bringing Sally to town & my Wishes & yours to be guided by their Judgment; told her that not being able to see Mr. B. she had been heard by such & such people who had given such & such opinions, which I w^d

not decide upon until I had seen them—in short urg'd a speedy meeting, endeavour'd to interest them for our Little Girl; directed to Mr. or Mrs. B; beg'd an answer from him if she was not in town & entreated he w^d procure for me a Means of her hearing ye Concert of Antient Music on Wednesday. John brought word Mrs. Bates is expected in town on thursday & he was not in. I believe it is only business that keeps him from his friends & hope I shall hear from or see him. In the meantime as you seem to think it best Sally sh'd not be taken to parties I will stop my hand, but must tell you that she gains universal applause produced in y^o manner she is, as one in *training* for ye Profession under my Protection, & it w^d certainly secure to her many friends & patrons when ever she does come out, but there is not one single person amongst all who have heard & admired her who does not think her much too young, too weak in Voice & Constitution & too Artless, in her manner of singing to make any figure as a professional singer at this time, & that it w^d Ruin her future interests to be produced as such. Y^e Plan I was going upon is generally approved. That she cuts down most, or suppose all, of ye Ladie singers is no proof that she is fit for ye Publick. But except to-morrow to Ld Camden & at Nelly's little Party on Saturday which she has made on purpose for her I will not let her be heard till she has past her Examination with ye Bates. As to her receiving gratuities at present I have many insurmountable objections to it. . . .

2 *o'Clock Tuesday.*—Just return'd from a quiet walk in ye Park with Sally to mend a shabby head. . . . I send you a satisfactory Letter [from Bates] which has

accompany'd 2 Tickets for y* Antients to-morrow, so I shall go with Sally myself. . . .

Wednesday morn⁹.—Lord C. [Camden] was much pleased with our Little Syren, said much in praise of her taste & growing Powers, admired but Liked not 'Caro Luci vi dire etc.' I said she had not learnt Handel but sh'd try any song he pleased. He chose ' I know that my Redeemer etc.'—taught her the *true expression* etc. and was quite in his Element & whisper'd Lady D. that he sh'd be eternally oblig'd if I would some morning let her call & sing a song to Lady Eliz. Pratt who was too Ill to come out. I have promised she shall write you an Acc^t of all her proceedings on friday, but to-day & to-morrow will be fully taken up. Mortellari comes both days, we go to ye Antients with Mr. & Mrs. Cotton & she is preparing for her exhibition to Mr. Bates wch is to take place to-morrow Evening. You see we are *en train* and everything succeeds to my wish. I think Mortellari takes great pains & teaches her a great deal; his taste is delightful, she thinks so also. . . .

Thursday.—The Antients answer'd our Expectations in some points. We were all Eyes & Ears, the Orchestra very fine but ye Music too loud & the singing very bad. We certainly c^d have done better as to taste & Judgment, but it must require great strength to sing in a Room so crowded & so hot. We sat out of the way of winds and near ye Door, yet have both sad Headaches to-day. I am vext for Sally & wish I c^d take it all. I have given her a dose of Salts & hope that will mend her before ye evening. If not Mrs. Bates knows how to make allowances & we must appoint another Day. . . . Ned had what I must call a fortunate Headach & was forc'd to come home from ye house to Bed at 9 o'Clock last night. The Papers will tell you they sat till ½ past 4 this Morning without ye 2 Principals opening their Lips & then adjourned till to-day. Ned is well to-day & gone upon Duty; my head gets better, Sally says hers does ye same. . . .

Friday.—. . . Sally's head got quite well as soon as she had conversed a Little with the Bates. They both express'd themselves very kindly towards us & seem'd much interested for her. I told them it was my wish & design to have consulted them before anybody had heard her & I inform'd them in what manner & by whom she had been heard & ye General approbation she had met with. It seem'd to be their real opinion that she sang well enough to do herself & Late Master (who ought to have ye Credit of having so well grounded her) great honor, & that being introduced by me in a manner so respectable, assisted by her own engaging manners must gain her friends & protection, & the report of persons so great in Musical knowledge w^d make people eager to hear her when she launches out. We talk'd about ye difficulty of placing her which they express themselves strong upon but only in General terms. . . . I was pleas'd to find they approve of Mortellari & say he is ye 1st Master for finishing a singer. . . .

Saturday.—Nelly is so occupy'd with her Arrangm^ts for this Evening that I am forced to take ye whole post upon myself. . . . You shall hear ye proceedings of to-day by Monday's post. Lady Palmerston has politely left her Ticket [card] for Sally ye same as for us & desired me to Bring her. There are no professional People admitted;

only Lady Singers, amongst whom she will shine & gain great applause I am sure. Adieu.

Sunday.—In my Life I never saw so thorough a day of Rain as this has been. We thought it impossible to take Serv^{ts} & horses out & have not been to Chapel, but since Church have had a circle of Visitors to *correct* our *Gothic notions.* The Party went off well & charmingly last night. Did I tell you that Ned has put up a handsome Chadeliere in each of ye Rooms? which lighted them beautifully, & ye House appear'd most strikingly handsome, y^r 1st time it ever was show'd to such a number of people. They did not I believe exceed 50 & therefore c^d not make a Crowd though they all got into one Room. The Music was so attractive that not a Soul w^d play at Cards, so ye fine Drawing Room w^d hardly have been seen at all if Nelly had not (chiefly for ye Comfort of ye Music party) made ye Company enter through ye Drawing Room & shut up the entrance of ye Great Room near ye organ. So ye Music was at that end out of ye Way of ye Crowd if there had been any & I think it c^d hardly have sounded better in ye Arbury Hall. Mortellari saw ye preparations for a Concert when he came to give Fanny her Lesson in ye morning, & beg'd so hard that he might come & accompany his two Scholars that he c^d not be refused, & as we took care to explain to Everybody that he had given ye Girls only a few Lessons each, Poor Motta had ye whole Credit & praise Due for his pains, & it gives me pleasure that such ample Justice is done to his memory. Every soul, ye Bates included, say it is impossible for any body to be better taught than Sally has been. I wish you could have been amongst us last night your Ears w^d have been fully Gratified in every sense. She sung ' Ombre Amene ' ' Generosi Bretagne ' & a new Duett with Fanny most divinely, & her Manner & person was praised almost as much as her Voice. The General Opinion is that she will make a most Capital Singer in a year or two when she gets at her full strength, but everybody adds what a pity to send such a Sweet inocent Girl out of a happy & secure situation into such a Sea of Dangers as this town! If the Bates's w^d take her that might be obviated perhaps, but it will be a difficulty & a very delicate thing to manage. I shall however have it in my eye & will offer myself to spend another Evening with them, & desire them to let me send Sally in the morning to pass the whole day there. Her Good Temper & Manner may engage them to make some offer of ye kind we wish. After all this I am sorry to add that she has so bad a return of the Numbness in her Head that I do not take her to Lady Palmerston's this Evening. She only sung ye 3 songs I mention with intervals of near an hour between them, which confirms me in ye Opinion that it is a Nervous affection & proceeds now from ye great anxiety & desire to do well. But it proves at least that either ye Mind, Body or both are at present unequal to great exertion. She has been excessively Low all day & is now Lying upon ye Sopha by me in a sound sleep. Lady Vernon has been so good to send us 4 Tickets for Catches & Glees to-morrow at Ld Exeter's & writes that one of them is for Sally. Indeed she has ye same respect & attention from everybody as if she was my Daughter. People insist that it is due to her on my Acc^t & for her own unassuming behaviour which shows that she perfectly understands her own situation, & they give me credit on that score which I am not a little proud of. I rather scruple taking her to Lord Exeter's where she will not entertain but be entertain'd. Everybody agrees that she sh'd hear all kinds of good Music & as this is a kind quite new to her I do not think I shall withstand ye temptation if she is quite well to-morrow. . . .

This is Monday. . . . Sally looks better & is in better spirits to-day, but her head still feels numb'd & she is in doubt whether she can take her Lesson with Mortellari, so I shall say nothing to her of Lord Exeter's, particularly as Nelly thinks it more than probable that he will ask her to sing, as he heard her here on Saturday & was much pleased.

There was a very pick'd assembly last night at Lady P.'s not numerous but almost all grandees & connoisseurs, Dutchess of Cumberland etc. etc., Lady Clarges, Miss Harris, Miss Erskine etc. etc. The 3 last mention'd sung well, but I think *we* sh'd have shone amongst them. No professional people admitted there. Lady P. & many others express'd great disappointment that Sally c^d not come & hoped to see her another time. In short her fame is gone abroad almost equal to your expectations & much exceeding mine. The business I think is to feed ye desire of hearing her in this infant *state* as we call it, but not to make ye gratification too easy nor too Common. At the same time to cultivate for her ye friendship and protection of those whose patronage may be Essential to her when she comes out. I am convinced we sh'd have done her an injury had we produced her in any other way than this. Indeed the Bates's say it c^d not have been done whilst she is carry'd about & introduced by me. I think I have not minded Nelly's orders in this but I know you are interested as much as I am for my Little Charge. . . .

Tuesday 6th March.—. . . I am sorry to say that Sally's numbness lasted all Sunday & yesterday & went off in ye night with an excruciating headach, which still continues tho' not so violent. She says she feels as if her Voice was quite gone, but I hope that is only fancy. I have sent for Evans & expect him every minute. He has been & she has told her own story to him fully & sensibly, & has confess'd having had those numbed sensations after singing much oftener than she has told both before she came to town & since. He confirms my opinion of its being nervous but speaks of ye Consiquences as being more serious than I apprehended. He does not absolutely object to her singing or learning to Sing if she can do it without difficulty & as it were in Sport, but on no consideration must her mind be agitated with hope or fear. He orders her Valerian & to steam her head over Rosemary & says he will see her again in a day or two. I have follow'd him out of ye Room to know his real opinion & he has frighten'd me sadly. He says her nerves seem to be very delicate & that she has a Scorbutic irritability about her, that must be prevented fixing there by taking care to keep her in an even tranquil state of Mind; that he has known Girls at her Age with ye Like delicate sensations lose all power of voice, even of speech, have a Paralytic Stroke or become stupify'd from great exertion of Spirits. No doubt these little Tryals before Company have been such to our Dear Girl & the Applause she has met with must Elivate her above herself, tho' she has appear'd Collected & unmov'd. But there must be an End of them, this year at least ; which will be a great disappointment to many & mortify me very much. I went yesterday to ye Bates & fixt to have another snug Evening with them on Friday & I was to send Sally to spend ye Day with them. They Promis'd to teach her ye Stile of singing Handel & Mrs Bates said she w^d practice duetts with her for ye Evening. I have just told Sally that I dare not venture upon this engagem^t. She answers ' indeed I am not at all afraid of M^r & Mrs Bates, they are so good natured to me & I am sure they won't let me Sing too much, for they don't think I am strong enough & they say it will Spoil my Voice.' I meant to give you 3 words & have fill'd my Paper with her.

Thursday.—. . . I am sure I frightened you as much as myself about our sweet little Syren. Her Letter yesterday I hope w^d calm your Mind as to present Danger but I am still uneasy. The Newdigates think she looks ill & she certainly is *Abbatue* & sung so faintly with Mortellari yesterday that I have forbid his coming again till Saturday & will not let her sing a note to-day. She begs so hard to spend ye day with ye Bates to-morrow that I consent on condition that she tells him all that has happened. Cards like ye enclosed were given to us all at Breakfast this morning. I did not observe at first that Sally had one till she gave it me with eyes streaming. I told her I sh'd determine nothing till ye day came & sh'd be guided by Evans's opinion. She will be hurt if she does not go, but I am afraid of so anxious a moment. Your Letter is just arrived. I am glad you seem to think so lightly of her Complaint. I have felt ye effect of nerves too severely not to dread it, but I will be guided by better & more impartial judgm^t than my Own. . . . I will be seeking out a Piano forte. I suppose you w^d have a New one if I can't get a good one second hand?

Saturday.—. . . Maberley is just gone from me, but I sh'd tell you 1st what I am sure you think most material, that my Cold is a vast deal better & that our sweet little Warbler was able to do herself great credit at ye Bates's yesterday. Her Voice was not strong but sweet as possible & they are quite astonish'd with her knowledge of Music & facility in reading it. She had learnt to sing & accompany a very difficult Duett of Handels & Mrs Bates & she sung it divinely. I must get her those Chamber Duetts & also Handel's Opera Songs in Score & ye Accompanyments to the 5 Vols. of oratorio Songs. She did not force her Voice but Mrs Bates says she sung a good Deal in ye course of ye day & feels no inconvenience from it. If she gets well in this day & to-morrow I will be guided by her opinion & wishes in regard to taking her to Lady Palmerston's. If she can do herself Creditt without injury to herself it may be a great thing for her, but I won't tell her how material, nor what Judges she is likely to see there; only prepare her for seeing a great Many People & tell her that if she is not quite certain she can sing to them with as Little fear as to ye Bates's I will not take her. Bates's give us great hopes of seeing them at Arbury this year, but I will leave Sally to tell you that on Monday. . . . Evans has just been here, finds his patient much mended. I hope with Care we shall not want further Advice. . . .

Tuesday 2 o'Clock.—I have been sitting two hours to Lawrence which I grumble at as I thought ye Picture was finish'd but Ned will have still another sitting on friday. . . . Nelly & I have both got bad Colds. She nursed hers last night & I chaperon'd ye two Girls to Lady Palmerstons. Y^e company was less numerous than last Week but very much Pick'd in ye Musical & tonish line. Sally sung ye Harp Song which Fanny accompany'd & gain'd very great applause tho' her Voice failed so much at ye end I was afraid she w^d not have got through it. I gave everybody to understand that she had been Ill & that ye faillure (which I believe few people were sensible of) was from weakness of Nerves. As soon as she had finish'd Lady P. came & took her by the hand, Complimented her upon her performance, led her into ye other Room to sit quiet & with her own Hand fetch'd her a Glass of water. She very soon recovered herself. Lady P. desired her not to sing any more if it w^d hurt her & I was afraid of her doing it, but not sorry to find that Applause had its proper effect in exciting ambition. She was very anxious to sing a Song she has learnt of Mortellari, so I gave way & to be sure never anything was so admir'd. It did shew her Voice, taste & Powers wonderfully & is the Stile of this frittering age, very pretty indeed if it is executed so neatly as she does it, but more graced than Poor Motta would have taught her. But as ye Bates observe: the plain Eligant Stile will not go down with ye greater number & she must please All. It is necessary to learn it & it is a fine exercise, she may leave it out when she will. She has a Little Head Ach to-day but not enough to make us put off Mortellari who comes at 8 this Evening. I will certainly consult any Physician for her you Approve but indeed Evans' opinion so perfectly coincides with my own that it satisfys me & ye Effect of ye Valerian & indeed every circumstance since he saw her has proved him in ye right. He says the less is done ye Better, now & then a Little Physic & valerian when she is nervous & either Harrogate or Cheltenham some time in ye summer. This he thinks will make her stout, but if it does not all we wish, the fault will be in her natural Constitution, which tho' not a bad one is irritable & he does not think any Course of medicine w^d alter it, but if injudiciously given might injure her very materially. Nelly tells me that for young Women Sir Lucas Peppys is in great Name. Indeed I do believe he has restored Fanny by forbidding all Medicine & keeping her in a Course of Air & Exercise. She has not had a Single Complaint since she came to town & is quite fat. . . .

Saturday night.—. . . They are all gone to the play except myself & Sally who has had ye head ach all day. . . . I will not answer the 1st part of your Letter my Dear Soul. I trust that we do perfectly understand each other's meaning tho' we may some times mistake an expression. If I have used any that were absurd or incoherent forgive it. My thoughts have frequently been wholely taken up with subjects far different from what I was writing about. Never suspect me of wanting confidence in you. But no more of this. . . .

Tuesday morn^g 9 o'Clock.—It will be a hurrying busy day. Little News [Newdigates] breakfast with us & will be going I dare say till near one, Mortellari comes at 11. I must settle with & pay him. Sir Lucas before 12 . . .

then I must carry Sally with me to Hollands to fix about ye Piano forte etc. I have seen several very good ones at Broderip's & Elsewhere at 18 & 20 guineas. Y^e new ones are raised now to 26 every where. . . .

3 *o'Clock*.—Newdigates set out in good Spirits about 1, mean to go to Rochester; they desire me to give love & thanks to Arbury. . . . They were all hurry but will write from Dover or Callais. . . .

Sir L. P. stay'd an hour & took great pains about Sally. He gives me great Comfort, thinks almost all her Complaints proceed from debility mearly temporary. He has given me a plan for her & talks so reasonably that I feel Confidence in his Assurances that all will go well.

2 *o'Clock Saturday.*—I have done all my Business, pack'd up all my things, spent all my Money. . . . I return as I came with an Empty place in ye Coach. If I c^d have brought Sally down it w^d have been worth while to have taken her out of ye house [in Spring Gardens] before ye regular time but I had promised her a week with a friend out of town & as she has had such an uncomfortable time, done so well & may never come up again I c^d not disappoint her to save her Carriage. . . . God bless you & grant us a happy Meeting before Dinner on Monday. . . .

CHAPTER X

1792—1795

The truth is that with one exception Caterina's only talent lay in loving; and there it is probable the most astronomical of women could not have surpassed her. Orphan and protégée though she was, this supreme talent of hers found plenty of exercise at Cheverel Manor, and Caterina had more people to love than many a small lady and gentleman affluent in silver mugs and blood-relations.—MR. GILFIL'S LOVE-STORY.

WE hear no more of a professional future for the little syren. Her organisation, physical and mental, was evidently unsuited for the trials and excitements of a public career, however successful it might have been. After her return from London in 1792 her health continued to give cause for much anxiety to her kind patrons, and we gather from contemporary letters that as the summer wore away, fears arose lest she should fall into a consumption. To avert this danger it was proposed to send her for the winter to Lisbon, then popular as a health resort owing to its mild climate and accessibility by sea. Sir Roger and Lady Newdigate spared no pains to find a suitable escort for the delicate girl and a home to receive her on her arrival at Lisbon. Lord Bagot was one of those to whom they applied for advice and assistance in this matter, and he ends a letter to Sir Roger on business affairs in the following manner:

So much for this disagreable subject, but it is only to go to another disagreable one, the dear Siren; whose Case I most sincerely lament. My Wife nor I have neither Lisbon connections nor knowledge of anybody likely to go thither. I am glad you have written to the Bishop of St Asaph on the subject. He or Mrs. Bagot may very likely be able to be of assistance & I am sure will be happy to be so if they can.

You told me last year you wo'd come to Blithfield this by water. Why are you not here? there has been no other method of coming even if you had embarked in an air Baloon.

This must be all Lady Newdigate's fault. She hear'd you make the promise & agree'd to it & now She will not come. There is no depending upon Women, but if you do not both come in the course of the Autumn I shall not put up with it. There are strange alterations since you were here. Perhaps Mrs. Bowdler (to whom & to her Daughter I beg my best Comp^{ts} & congratulate you upon having been able to keep them so long, for here they were very volatile) may have told you it is become a tolerable looking place out of doors. I have brought my Park & Woodlands to my House, & made Savanahs upon the Blythe that you can see no end of. But I know what wo'd bring you here sooner than all I co'd shew you, if I co'd do it : viz. tell you how happy you wo'd make us if you wo'd come. Talk about it to my Lady. She may have some conscience left & let us hear about it.

All here join in love to All at Arbury
I am dear Sir Roger ever
Yours most affectionately
BAGOT.

Blithfield
Augst 24, 1792.

In the course of the autumn Sally was sent to Lisbon under the charge of a Mr. and Mrs. Close, and one of her letters from thence is here given. It is written to Sir Roger, and is dated

April y*e* 9th 1793
Braco de Prata.

SIR,—I hope you will pardon and forgive me in delaying writing to you so long. I assure you it was not from disinclination that I did not answer your very kind letter sooner, but merely from not knowing properly how to express my Gratitude to you for your good advice, which indeed has been of great service to me. It is impossible ever to repay you and Lady Newdigate for all the trouble and expence that you have been at to re-establish my health, but I hope by the assistance of God I shall soon recover it. I assure you I have him always in my thoughts and without him nothing can be done. I depend on him for the recovery of my Health and I flatter myself that he will succeed. I have laid up all youthful flights and attend solely to my health. Indeed that would be very unpardonable in me if I had not attended to it, after all the trouble that you have been at in sending me so far from all my Friends; but I am not without Friends where ever I go. I don't know the reason of it, but it is very fortunate for me. Indeed you have no Idea how good and attentive Doctor Withering has been to me. How very lucky I have been in being in the same house with him and amongst such rational society. Musick goes on pretty well but I have not much time to practice as we are so large a party. Mrs. Close sings most evenings and a most delightful pipe she has. We do not yet sing Duetts together as Doctor Withering will not allow me to try my voice till the first of May. French goes on very rapidly. Mr. Close is so good and kind as to give up to us an hour every day and sometimes two. He gives us English Exercises to turn into French and indeed we work very hard at it. We are studing it most part of the day. Miss Pearson and Miss Penelope learnt it for two years at School and they ought to know a great deal more than we do, but Mr. Close says that we are all much the same. I flatter myself that I shall be able to converse with you when I return which I hope will be very soon. Doctor and Miss Withering intend leaving this Kindom about the 26th of May in the How Packet and I hope I shall have a Letter from my Good and almost only Friend that I have in the World to tell me whether I stay or go. I hope it will be the Latter as I think it a very long time since I have seen you. I suppose I shall find Arbury a very different place from when I left it; there will be so many improvements that I shall not know it. I often think what you are doing and how I used to imploy my time, tho' I am afraid that I did not imploy it properly very often. I have often thought of the hours that I lost when I might have been improving myself. Indeed I am very much surprized how Lady Newdigate could have so much patience in teaching me any thing, for I was very stupid and Lazy. Certainly nobody could have had the opportunities of making the greatest improvement in everything as I have had. I have written a long Letter to Miss Willoughby and told her everything. This Packet sails to-morrow and I have sent by it half a Chest of Oranges for Mrs. Oliver. I hope they will get safe to her and be good ones. There are scarcely any good ones to be had here, tho' they are so plentiful. We give four hundred and eighty reas a hundred of Oranges which is in english money 2s. 8½d.

I will give you a description of our habitation; it is situated by the side of the River which is twelve miles broad and there are some beautiful hills that are beyond it. If I was a drawer I would bring home the whole Country. The house stands rather in a Wood and the Garden is upon a hill where there is a summer house that takes in the whole Country. Below it there is a most beautiful Wood where we stroll and all the young people except Master Henry Close and myself study Botany in it. Doctor W. instructs them and they like it very much. The Nightingales are beginning to sing and they make the wood their Theatre where they all meet in an evening and treat us with a few of their sweet tunes. The Black Birds are beginning but they are not so fine as ours. Doctor Withering Mr. Close and Mr. Pearson are going to the Caldas next Friday. Doctor W. has got permission from government to try a Chemical experiment on the Waters which will be a very good thing for the Physicians do not know their qualities.

We are all invited to a Masquerade which will be as soon as the Princes of Brasils is brought to bed which is expected every day. Great preparations are getting ready against the event takes place and there are to be Illuminations Three nights. Doctor W. has proclaimed that I may go with Mr. C. and the young Ladies and that it will do me no harm. I assure [you] it was his own proposal, for I had no Idea that I should go. Please to present my Best Respects to Lady Newdigate and Compliments to all that I have the honour of knowing. We have had some very bad weather indeed, but we flatter ourselves that it is now set in for good. I have not been quite so well but I hope this fine weather will set us all up. I believe it is the water that disagrees with me for I have had a Violent Complaint in my Bowels, but I hope it is going off. I hope you will excuse my mentioning it to you.

It is reported and believed that the Queen is dead, but it is not to be known for certain till the Princes is brought to bed. . . . I am afraid the poor Piano forte will be very much out of tune.

I am Sir

Your ever grateful Dutiful

and much obliged

servant

S. SHILTON.

The little songstress, who was evidently becoming weary of her banishment, was permitted to return to England at the time she desired. She left Lisbon towards the end of May and reached Arbury in the month of June, much improved in health and spirits. On her arrival she found her kind patrons rejoicing at the news of the birth of a son and heir to the Charles Parkers at Harefield.

Joy to me my Dr Sir Roger [writes the happy father] & thanks to God for as fine a Boy as ever was seen, which our Dearest Jessy has just presented me with & all safe & well . . . before three She was deliver'd of this fine, fat Broad Shoulder'd Gentleman.

Pray God grant him Health & Life that he may see & know You & learn to respect & love You as his Father

Charles Parker.   Jane Anstruther,
                   wife of Charles Parker

does. . . . I have great Reason to be thankful for so happy an Event & I am sure you & Lady Newdigate will cordially partake of our Joy. . . .

Ever aff^{ty} Yours
CHARLES PARKER.

Harefield Lodge:
3 o'Clock Morning.

Sir Roger wrote a characteristic letter in reply, which has been preserved. It is addressed to the new-born infant, who received the names of Charles Newdigate.

To Master Charles Newdigate Parker

This I guess my dear little Boy is the very first Letter of congratulation addressed to you, on your fortunate arrival in this World, which probably you can neither read nor understand, but instruction cannot come too soon, and it is never too early to be wise! You have a great deal to do & the sooner you set about it the better.

The first lesson I shall give you is—Risu cognoscere Matrem—the only return yet in your power to make for the long tedious months she has passed for your good: Next you are to stretch out your little hands, both of them remember, & take Papa by the Chin, kiss him & Mamma till they laugh, for no good can come to him— Cui non risere Parentes. I don't explain this as I conclude your knowledge in all languages is the same.

Then look about you & you will probably find out a Grand Mamma, that in course of time will do her best to humor & spoil you: kiss her & thank her.

They will tell you of other Friends you have a long way off, that long to see you & expect you to come as soon as they will let you. Be sure to do this—to Nod your head & smile.

Enough for the present, you shall have more as you come to weeks & months of discretion, for tho' a hundred miles off & I have never seen you I feel a great Partiality for you, & so does a certain Lady near me, wishing you a long & happy Life to the joy & comfort of your dear Parents! Adieu.

Yours most affectionately
PÆDAGOGUS.

Nine months later Sir Roger, who was always ready to tender advice, be it concerning Sally's stays or the upbringing of infants, is again a scribe on the subject of this welcome baby's training. This time he writes as if from the child to its mother, the signature appearing from its irregular characters to have been traced by a pen held in the infant's own little fist.

MY DEAR MAMMA,—Take notice that if, after the receit of the inclosed you shall fail to give me cold water to roll in every morning and the best of milk & a good deal of it, all day long, and a stout nimble nurse to toss me about from morning till evening from the date hereof till the first of January next I am advised to bring my Action against you, so pray Dear Mamma be careful of

Your loving Son
CHARLES NEWDIGATE PARKER.

Arbury 26 of
March 1794.

These are specimens of Sir Roger's correspondence in his lighter moods. He could also administer a dignified rebuke when the occasion demanded it. He has kept rather a curious correspondence with a lady who was one of the last representatives of the old family of Ashby of Breakspears, near Sir Roger's Harefield property in Middlesex. The Ashby family had a burying-place called the Breakspears Chapel in Harefield Church. The living of Harefield being what is known as 'a peculiar,' the patron of it was possessed of more than ordinary power in connection with the edifice and surrounding churchyard, a privilege which Sir Roger clung to with the natural tenacity of his character. Mrs. Ashby writes:

S^R,—Give me leave to Inform you I have put a Small Tablet of Marble in Memory of my Mother in a very Obscure part of Harefield Church by the Window near the Bells. As the Partridge family wou'd not admit my Sister who died in the year 1772 to be deposited in the Chapell my Mother after many Cruel Conflicts determin'd to be laid by her Children who were all denied Altho' the only petition they ever asked . . . the Inscription I enclose for your perusal, If it merits Praise or Blame its all my own, & shall esteem myself highly Obliged & honour'd by your Opinion & advice how to act in Consequence of a Prosecution against me by Mr. Partridge for telling the truth; I am perfectly ignorant of Law beyond the Commandments. . . . I shall wait with impatience to hear from you as expenses will increase. . . . Our Familys are both very Ancient & there has been great friendship between them. Permit me to offer Compts to Mrs. M. Conyers whom I shou'd be happy to see; I have a very comfortable habitation & the respect & kind attention of all my neighbours

& am Y^r oblig'd & most Obed^t

A. ASHBY.

Rickmansworth June 30th
1790

Inscription enclosed

TO THE MEMORY OF ANN ASHBY
VENERABLE IN LIFE, HIGH & GLORIOUS IN IMMORTALITY
DAUGHTER OF WHITLOCK BULSTRODE ESQ^{RE}
AND ELIZ. DINSLY HIS WIFE OF HOUNSLOW
AND WIFE OF W^M ASHBY ESQ^{RE} OF BREAKSPEARS
(WHO WAS THE SON & HEIR OF FRANCIS ASHBY & JUDITH TURNER
HIS WIFE)
BY WHOM SHE HAD THREE DAUGHTERS
ANNE, CHARLOTTE & REBECCA
SHE DEPARTED THIS LIFE JULY 28 1785
AGED 93
HERE ALSO LYES THE BODY OF REBECCA ASHBY
WHO DEPARTED THIS LIFE JULY 12TH 1772
ON THE DECEASE OF THE ABOVE MENTION'D W^M ASHBY ESQ^{RE}
THE FAMILY ESTATE DESCENDED TO HIS YOUNGER BROTHER
WHOSE DAUGHTER POSSESS'D IT DURING THE LIFE TIME
OF THE WIDOW & CHILDREN OF THE AFORESAID W^M ASHBY.
BUT WOULD NOT ADMIT THEIR REMAINS TO
REST IN THE CHAPELL WITH THEIR ANCESTORS
O READER THINK ON THIS.

Sir Roger's Answer

MADAM,—I am favor'd with your Letter & beg leave to inform you that no one has any right to erect monuments in the Church of Harfield without my permission by my Commissioner Sir W. Scott. This I conclude you was ignorant of as I heard nothing from you before.

If I had been ask'd my opinion of the inscription before you put it up, I sh'd have told you very freely that I c^d not recommend the recording Family differences on Marble to Posterity; that I sh'd be happy at all times to be an instrument in reconciling my neighbours when at variance, but beg to be excused taking a part myself. From your Letter I can give no opinion of the Prosecution carried on against you wch you mention & heartily wish—which is all I can do—for a restoration of Peace in your Family & amongst all my neighbours.

    I am Madam
      Y^r most obedient servant
Arbury: ROGER NEWDIGATE.
July 5th 1790.

We must now return to the summer of 1794 to quote a letter to Sir Roger from Mr. Mundy, giving a graphic account of the arrival of the news of Lord Howe's great victory over the French on June 1 of that year. The tidings of that welcome success were brought to the opera by Lady Chatham, whilst the performance was going on, and it was at once announced to the large audience there assembled.

The only date on Mr. Mundy's letter is the day of the week—Wednesday.

MY DEAR SIR,—I cannot resist the Temptation of wishing you all Joy of our great and splendid Victory at Sea, and fearing your Paper might be silent upon it or not give you the particulars as far as are at present known I put down on paper what transpired last night on Sir Roger Curtis's arrival.

Lord Howe had two actions with the French Fleet; in the last on ye 1st of June he brought them to close Action and took seven Sail of Line of Battle Ships. Six are coming home; one sunk soon after she surrendered, and one is supposed to have gone down during the Engagement. Lord Howe laid the Queen Charlotte close on board the French Admiral and in a very short time gave him so good a beating that he set every sail he could and ran out of his Line, leaving his fleet to shift for themselves. Admirals Bowyer and Pasley and Cap^tn Nutt have each lost a Leg; Adm¹ Graves wounded in the arm and Cap^tn Montague killed. No further particulars are yet known; except that several more french ships were so much damaged, they did not think they could reach Brest. Admiral Montague with 9 sail of fresh line of Battle Ships is gone off Brest and it is expected he will give some acc^t of their crippled fleet running into harbour. Ld Howe is coming home, his ship having lost a mast, but he has left all his well-condition'd Ships to pursue.

We received this News last night at the Opera where Mortichelli was singing a favorite song. She was silenced in a Moment, and Rule Britannia called for, which was repeated at least a dozen times, the Audience all standing and huzzaing.

As I was in the next box to Lady Chatham who brought the news to us, I had the pleasure of announcing to Sir Wm Howe the first intelligence of his Brother's success. The poor Man could not utter a word for many minutes he was so overcome with Joy.

I don't find the name of l'Aigle in Ld Hood's letter, therefore suppose she was cruising. I have not heard from George [1] lately.

We go on well in Derbyshire with our subscription and have determined to raise a Body of Cavalry consisting of Gentlemen and Yeomen. Sir H. Harpur, Sir Robt Wilmot, Maj^r Bathurst, Cap^tn Cheney and I have already offered our services.

God bless you all
Your affectionate
E. M. MUNDY.

[1] Mr. Mundy's third son, afterwards Admiral Sir George Mundy, K.C.B.

Sir Roger's happiness in the birth of a son to his favourite cousin, Charles Parker, received an overwhelming shock in the unexpected death of the father, before the child was two years old. In the month of April 1795 Charles Parker was laid up with a cold accompanied by fever. For this he was bled, in accordance with the practice of the time. Delirium set in, followed by a sudden collapse, and he passed away when only thirty-nine years of age. He left behind him a widow and five young children, four of them girls, and an only son. The latter, Charles Newdigate Parker, succeeded to Harefield, and in accordance with Sir Roger's will took the name and arms of Newdegate instead of those of Parker. He married early Maria, daughter of Ayscoghe Boucherett, Esq., of Willingham in Lincolnshire, but died in 1833, before his fortieth birthday. He left an only child, the late Right Honourable Charles Newdigate Newdegate, of Arbury and Harefield, member for North Warwickshire for forty-two consecutive years. Mr. Newdegate died on April 10, 1887, and with him passed away the last descendant of Charles Parker.

CHAPTER XI

1795

Sir Christopher was listening with polite attention to Lady Assher's history of her last man-cook, who was first-rate at gravies, and for that reason pleased Sir John—he was so particular about his gravies was Sir John: and so they kept the man six years in spite of his bad pastry.

Lady Cheverel and Mr. Gilfil were smiling at Rupert the bloodhound, who had pushed his great head under his master's arm and was taking a survey of the dishes, after snuffing at the contents of the Baronet's plate.

Mr. Gilfil's Love-story.

IN the summer of this year, 1795, Lady Newdigate was suffering from an affection in one of her knees, which crippled her and caused her much pain. She was advised on this account to try a change of air and sea-bathing, and set out from Arbury for the south coast early in the month of August. Her first destination was Stansted Park in Sussex, at that time in the possession of a rich Indian nabob, Mr. Barwell by name. After her arrival there she was to decide between the rival claims of various untried places on the coast.

Mr. and Mrs. Barwell had been constant and kind friends to Lady Newdigate's sister, Mrs. Barton, and her scapegrace of a husband, and thus earned the gratitude and friendship of the Mundy family. Mrs. Barwell was a great favourite with everyone, and Lady Newdigate often speaks of her in her letters as 'the Sweet Little Woman,' or the 'Little Angel.' Many years later, in 1811, Mr. Mundy married Mrs. Barwell, then a rich widow, as his third wife.

Lady Newdigate's sister, 'Milly' Barton, was her companion on this expedition to Sussex. The latter was at this time so frequent a resident at Arbury, with her young daughter Nelly, but without her husband, that it seems probable the Mundy family had managed to provide for Mr. Barton elsewhere, much to the comfort of his immediate belongings.

The only other family event to be chronicled before beginning Lady Newdigate's fresh batch of letters is the marriage of her niece Fanny, Mr. Mundy's only daughter by his first marriage. Her wedding took place in June of this summer, the bridegroom being Lord Charles FitzRoy, second son of the third Duke of Grafton. Henceforth Fanny Mundy is spoken of as Lady Charles. Mrs. Nelly Mundy still remained with her brother as the mistress of his house.

Lady Newdigate and Mrs. Barton started in two carriages from Arbury, with their usual accompaniments of male and female servants, and both being in delicate health their first day's journey was a short one, to Walton, Sir John Mordaunt's place in Warwickshire.

Here are only [Lady Newdigate writes] Sir John, Lady M. & ye six girls who all *pet* me as much as you and Nelly do, but are *less severe* than ye latter. . . . Mrs Barton found an answer from Mrs Grayham about ye Little Bathing Place near Brighton; she recommends it for sea-bathing and driving, but she says there is no opportunity of going out in Boats, nor does she know that there are hot Baths. Lady Willoughby is just come from Cows & Lady M. will desire her to call here to-morrow to give an Acc^t of that Place. Sir John says that Royalty & ye great encampment has frighten'd many from Brighton this year, & she supposes there is less company there than almost any place upon that Coast, but these circumstances must make it disagreable. . . .

The travellers' next stopping-place was at Woodstock, two days later, and on Sunday they reached Walliscote, where they stayed with the Cottons. (Mrs. Cotton was a Conyers, and related to Sir Roger's first wife.) Lady Newdigate continues:

I have gained much since I set out, the swelling of my knee abates daily . . . & I c^d walk upon even ground without a stick but think it not safe to do so. . . . I am not fatigued at all by ye 30 miles drive of yesterday which indeed was delicious, neither Wind nor Sun to molest us, ye Road smooth & Country most beautiful. The Phaeton is indeed ye most delightful Vehicle for such an expedition that is possible. If ease of body & mind are essential ingredients in this prescription I am sure I have them in perfection, thanks to my dear Sir Roger and to those on whose care I can depend that he shall have no wants or wishes in my absence, but that we may all meet again in health & comfort. . . . We think to get to Farnham to-morrow, 29 miles, from whence we have about 27 to Stanstead, Charming Easy days, the Poneys came in as fresh last night as if they had gone no more than our usual airing.

Stansted Wednesday morning.—Here we are safe & well, have had a most delightful Journey. I never quited the Phaeton ye whole way & Milly only for a couple of hours ye night before last, when having the Misfortune to deserve ye Name of misguided travellers we got into Cross Roads & did not arrive at our destination till nine o'Clock. To be sure now it is over it is quite laughable and a good Lesson to reflect how many Scrapes one little détour might have led us into & how many superfluous miles we have gone to avoid ye inconveniencies that w^d otherwise have attended it. You might observe from ye Contrary Routes that Milly & I sent you from Walliscote that we were wavering as to our Plan. Y^e sisters were decidedly for going thro' Reading & Farnham, but Mr Cotton from Consultation of Maps & Conversation with Postillions believ'd it w^d be full as good & pleasant

& a much shorter Road to go by Basingstoke & Alton. In y^c first of these places we found it 19 miles instead of 15 & were inform'd that instead of 10 miles good turnpike to Alton there was not above 3 miles made & ye rest so Cut as to be impassable for such a Carriage as mine; In short that we had 12 miles cross country Road. We were only 17 miles good turnpike from Winchester; that w^d have been our sensible plan, but our Evil Genius had got possession of ye day. Y^e Landlord of ye house told me y^c Road was equally good to Alresford & that we sh'd there be 10 miles nearer to Stanstead. We listen'd to him & y^c Consiquence was we had 8 miles Bad Road out of 16 & was an hour in ye dark. But ye Poneys perform'd wonders & we were perfectly well & happy in the thought that our difficulties were over. But behold ye 15 miles good Road which we were inform'd w^d take us to horndean turn'd out 19 of quite impassable. The only good way was by Wickam & that by a détour of 20 miles, then by another détour of 14 miles to Havant & then 4½ to Stansted. But this was a misfortune only to y^c poor Poneys who in fact made nothing of ye 38½ miles, but came in as fresh as possible, & to be sure we had a variety of y^c most beautiful scenes the whole day that was possible & came over Post Down which is directly over Portsmouth & commands a full view of Spithead. I was delighted but it was 8 o'Clock before we got to Stansted, rather too dark to see y^c approach in perfection, but it had a magnificent appearance. Y^c family were all enjoying ye sweet evening in ye portico & welcom'd us very cordially.

. . . Y^c company here consists of Mrs. Barwell's 2 Sisters, 2 Ladies whose names I have not yet learnt & 4 or 5 men, all Indians I believe. The hours of ye family are what ye Polite World w^d not conform to viz. Breakfast at 8½, dine at 3½, supper at 9 & go to bed at 10, but everybody is at Liberty to order Breakfast, Dinner or Supper into their own Rooms & no questions ask'd. . . . The amendment of my Leg is really like a charm. . . . I walk firm & secure & gain strength in ye Joynt. In other respects I am well except want of sleep, which makes me feel Languid & headachy in a Morning. . . . I never closed my eyes till 5 and wak'd again before 7. Sea air alone I doubt will not break ye spell. I hope ye warm Bath will. Most of this company are earnest for ye Isle of Whight but we determine upon nothing until we hear from Mrs Graeme who is to send us a full Acc^t from Worthing of that place.

2 *o'Clock.*—I have had a most enchanting drive thro' ye Park & Cuts thro' ye forest. Mrs B. is so good to propose a Jaunt to Portsmouth & ye Isle of Wight tomorrow if ye Weather is like to-day, & has also bespoke me a Water Cart of Sea Water which Nanny Ashcroft has undertaken to have properly heated & put into a most convenient Bath here. Baths in ye house of all sorts. One may be Stew'd in Vapour, Boil'd & Wash'd in any way one pleases, so you see I am losing no time by this Agreable Visit.

Thursday morning 10 *o'Clock.*—. . . Our expedition is put off on acc^t of dear Milly's Ear; it has given her a bad night. . . . Mrs Barwell is going to take me to Up Park, Sir H. Featherstone's. Oh what good news I have to tell you! Nanny Ashcroft got me ye most delightful & perfect Warm Sea Bath last night at 9 o'Clock, after

W^{ch} I ate my Bason of Milk & went to Bed. . . . I believe I was asleep before 2 & never waked till 7, am free from Head Ach, perfectly cool & comfortable & my Knee so strong & well that I have been up stairs to see Milly & all over ye Principal Appartments of this superb Palace. . . .

Friday morn^g ½ past 9.—. . . What a noble situation has Up Park! but the air was hazy, we c^d hardly distinguish the Sea. Y^e Woods very fine & coming down apace; much may be spared if taken judiciously but I fancy ye possessors Judgment is chiefly in horses, & the only object to feed them. The day was heavenly & we just got back before a storm of thunder began; it was not near us, but ye Lightning Vivid & incessant all afternoon & all night. To-day is Gloomy & pleasant & Mr Barwell promises fine Weather so we resolve not to delay an expedition plan'd last night to Bognor Rocks, a place strongly recommended to us about 16 miles from hence. I was to have taken Mrs Barwell in my Phaeton & one of her sisters to have taken Milly in her Curricle, but alass Milly's Ear is not broke & it w^d be folly for her to venture. So Mrs Brown only accompanies me with John & a serv^t of Mrs Barwell's who knows ye place to attend us. The Efficacy of ye 1st Sea Bath was for one night only. I have had Little Sleep but am well & my Leg gains strength. The Little Angel will give me another Bath to-morrow. . . .

From Mrs. Barton

MY DEAR SIR ROGER,—Lady New. has left me her Letter to finish. . . . She seems perfectly well . . . except in respect to Sleep. . . . I find she has told you of my ill-behaviour. 'Tis a Vile Ear & torments me sadly. ... I must be very careful to prevent a return of it. Mrs Colbeck assures me that a little bit of *Negro's Wool* will effect it, and has offered me a bit of *her Black* Serv^ts Head. But I don't know whether I can persuade myself to try it. I should think a bit of Sheep's Wool wou'd do as well & be a much sweeter thing. ... We are certainly well accommodated here and the dear Little Angel and her Caro Sposo are as attentive as possible to make everything pleasant and Convenient, but my dear Companion and I will not be sorry for more quiet. Our Numbers are great & the Male part of Barwell's Guests not exactly the Men one wou'd wish to pass a Summer with; but we see little of them except at Meals, as the chief pleasure they find in this Beautiful place is walking round the Billiard Table. Major Balfour (one of the party) has been here four years running for a month at a Time & has never set his foot beyond the Colonade. Why do such people come into the country? ... Your little Angel & Mr B. desire their best Comp^ts Adieu.

From Lady Newdigate

Sunday morning 17*th August.*—. . . Mr Barwell has Just told Milly that ye Clergyman is taken Ill & can give no Service, so he says it will be a Writing Day with everybody & advises that we sh'd let him have our Letters soon, least his number [1] sh'd be full. Milly is better but not quite free from Ear Ach. I am glad she did not go with us to Bognor for we dined upon ye Beach wch w^d not have suited her so well as it did Mrs Barwell & me

---

[1] For franking.

who were quite delighted with the Place. Sir Richd Hotham to whom it belongs has built 30 or 40 neat convenient Houses of different sizes for ye reception of Company, all pleasantly situated & with full view of ye Sea. A convenient Hot Sea Bath is also just made, & the Great World has taste enough to prefer it to all others upon this Coast. Whilst we sat at dinner there pass'd the Duchesses of Devonshire & Rutland, Lady E. Foster, Dow^{ger} Lady Sefton etc. & we saw ye Names & Titles of at least 20 more of ye very supreme set. At first it deterr'd me from enquiring about Lodgings notwithstanding ye various Comforts & Advantages we sh'd derive from being only 16 miles from this Hospitable family, but on Considering ye thing more seriously it appear'd evident to me that ye houses c^d not be occupy'd by any Company that w^d promise us such perfect ease & solitude. They are much too fine to Notice us, we sh'd be amused with seeing them drive about & they will insure us a good Supply of provisions, tho' perhaps we may pay a Little Dearer for them. This reasoning produced an immediate summons to ye Woman who has ye Letting of ye Houses. She at 1st said there was not one of any size vacant, but at last own'd that one very small one, 4 guineas p^r Week, was just given up, but that a Lady had secured ye refusal of it. We went to see it & it is so perfect a Little Cabin that I am quite wild to have ye Ladies answer. How we shall all squeeze into it I can't tell, for ye whole Consists of 2 Little Parlours in one of which there is a Bed; above a little Dining Room & Bed Chamber; over that 2 bed Chambers & below a Kitchen & Scullery. Bill must have a Bed at ye Inn with his horses, & the 2 Men have y^e

Parlour, but how shall we do for house maid & Cook? Betty in this case turns out a great Convenience. Neither she nor Barret make any difficulties; they say that with a Woman to help adays, who is recommended by ye Old Lady who promised us all assistance they shall do very well & we can hire everything we want either at ye Rocks or at Chichester which is only 7 miles distant & in ye direct road from this place, so that I am sure we shall want for nothing.

I was upon Wallerton Down yesterday & round by Ld George Lenox's Park, a beautiful Road & fine view of Spit H^d & ye Isle of W^{te}. When we shall get to either I know not for I cannot bear to go without Dear Milly. Indeed she says she has promised you not to trust me so long out of her sight. If I could Conquer bad nights I do feel that I sh'd be very frisky, but ye greatest perfection of a Bath (wch I had last night) did not answer so well as ye 1st tryal. I had very little Sleep . . . but feel well to-day & am going to drive Mrs Barwell in my Phaeton as it is a rule in this family that without necessity no horses go out on Sunday. But as we cannot pray & I am in pursuit of health I may transgress. . . .

Sunday night 11 *o'Clock.*—We are Rakes to-night, the Cause is this: Milly's Ear is quite Easy & the Weather so fine that we have been planning our expedition to Portsmouth for to-morrow. It will consist of 4 Ladies & 2 Gentlemen. Mr Barwell sends off by day break to bespeak ye best Boat & if ye Day is fine we are to go round the Fleet at Spit Head. Monsr le Comte de Narbonne Aid de Camp to Monsr D'Artois is on a visit to a Neighbouring family who brought him here this afternoon. He says Monsr is on board the Queen Charlotte at Spit Head, so possibly we may see him. We shall at Least Admire ye noble Ship he is in. We are to have breakfast & be off by ½ pst 9. I drive Mrs Barwell in my Phaeton & shall take both John & Thomas, ye former only was at Bognor. I made Bill bring ye Poneys down to ye sands & they let ye sea wash over their hoofs without sign of fear in them or their Rider. I perhaps shall not be able to add a Word in ye morning so God bless you.

Monday 12 *o'Clock.*—A Rainy Bad Day. . . . Milly has just told me that Comte de Narbonne & several Gents & Ladies dine here. I don't think I shall dine amongst them but feel quite equal to meeting them in ye Drawing Room. Have been settling Posting Acc^{ts} with John & what do you think ye Journey from Arbury here comes to? We paid 14^d per mile great part of ye way for ye Chaise horses & 6^d all ye way for ye saddle horse. Y^e whole, Baits & Sleepings included comes to above £24 to this place. A Dear Prescription but it is Doct^r & Apothecary too, & I must say has kill'd all my Dragons about my knee. At one time I began to fear I sh'd be a Cripple for Life. . . .

Wednesday morning.—All well & Jolly, Laughing & being Laugh'd at for our odd expedition of yesterday which upon ye whole delighted us & has done us all good. It was exactly comformable to Tapscots prescription, a little Rough sailing, sea spray but not sickness to agitate. We had a fine drive to Portsmouth & ye novelty of a fortify'd Place in England threw my Ideas into an agreable Confusion, but the Day turn'd out Windy &

Squally & our hearts began to fail us as to ye sailing part. Mrs Barwell who is a great Coward w^d go to ye platform & look out at ye Sea before she determin'd. I was passive being well assured we sh'd not venture foolishly. Mrs Barwell took fright when she saw ye Ruffled Ocean & ye Little Boat in which we were to pass to our Great Deck Boat, dance up & down & was coming back to ye Inn to consult about a Change of Plan, when she met Admiral Macbridge & Lady Lauderdale just arrived from Ryde & going to embark again for Cows. The former told her that it was just ye Weather that was pleasantest for Sailing in so safe a Boat as We had got; that they were merely on a sailing party of pleasure & were tempted to prolong it as the day was so favorable; but that we sh'd embark immediately as ye tide was going to turn. This report out weigh'd ye Dear Little Woman's fears & we set out, but I thought I never c^d have got into ye Boat. It was one instant even with ye Stairs, ye next 2 or 3 yards distant & as much below them. I gave myself up entirely to Mr Barwell Brown & two Able Sailors who handed me from one to ye other very Cleverly, & getting into ye great Boat was Easy as we had a strong side Wind & she Lay quite on one side. So far was happy & ye sight of ye Ships at Spit head magnificent. We sailed thro' ye midst of them both going & coming back, for I sh'd have told you we had determined to go over to ye Isle of W. The Wind was against us, we had frequent unpleasant Squalls which dash'd the Spray over us & we were oblig'd to tack many times which made all ye Company most Compleatly sick except Milly & myself. We sat upon deck all the time, cast a Wise look at each other from time to time & then Laught at ourselves & Companions. No one quitted ye Deck but Mrs Barwell who firmly resolv'd if it sh'd please God to Land her safe on ye Isle of W. that she w^d never quit that spot again. In an hour & half we accomplish'd ye 5 miles to Ryde, but ye Vessel could not get within a quarter of a Mile of the shore & ye getting into a small Boat was very disagreable & for me very difficult in so Rough a Sea, but my Knee gave no intimation of weakness. . . . We landed happily & Mrs B. Miss G. & Miss Impey immediately got well, but Miss Bell Barwell ye sweet Little Girl *you have heard us mention* continu'd so Ill we c^d not get her to Upper Ryde as we intended. So we took up our quarters just where we Landed at ye house of a Cousin of yours I suppose, a Mrs Stevens,[1] Little better than a Cottage but neat & comfortable. I talk'd to her of her descent & that of her husband, for I found they were of ye same name, but they did not seem to know that their Ancestors were ever in better plight. We all, except ye poor Girl, ate a good Cold Dinner & left her in a sound sleep in ye Care of Mrs Stevens whilst we walk'd about to see as much as we Could of the Island, a most rich & beautiful scene indeed, & strongly did Mrs Barwell urge the sending back for Cloaths & to inform Mr B. that we sh'd stay to go over y^e Island & till y^e Weather was fine. But y^e sailors told us the Wind w^d be in our favor & y^e Sea smooth & that $\frac{3}{4}$ of an hour w^d land us at Portsmouth. Y^e 1st & last were true, but y^e Wind in y^e Morning had occasion'd a great Swell & there being a dead Calm for some time we

---

[1] Mary, daughter of Sir Richard Newdigate, second baronet, had married William Stephens, Esq., of Barton in the Isle of Wight, in 1696.

were toss'd about & y^c 4 Ladies were again very sick, but Milly & I got used to ye Rolling & enjoy'd y^c fine sight of ye ships. We pass'd close by ye Comerrac de Marseilles, Y^e Prince of Wales, Glory & many other 1st rate M. of War & I suppose there are not fewer than 20 of that description at Spithead. Y^e Queen Charlotte we also saw, but not near enough to introduce ourselves to Monsr & ye Prince of W. stay'd we were told but 2 hours. It was a sweet evening for ye Phaeton & not dark tho' we did not get to Stansted till nine o'Clock. . . . I had ye enclosèd agreable note from Sir R. Hotham's factotum & we have determin'd to remove there [to Bognor] on Friday, not without much kind opposition from our host & hostess. Indeed we have every reason to leave them with regret but such a Cabin as we have got will have great Charms & our Menage will not be of a common Stamp. I have order'd a 2nd Bed in y^c Parlour that Bill may not be led into Evil by sleeping at ye Inn. . . .

From Mrs. Barton

Stansted 20*th August* (*Thursday*).—. . . Notwithstanding the attention & kindness we receive we are both of us ungrateful enough to wish to get into our little quiet Habitation to which we remove to-morrow. We send off our two maids and John as soon as we are dressed in the morning, mean to eat an early dinner here and be at Bognor at 6 to-morrow evening, that I may feast my eyes with a full Sea which it will be at that hour. I am not surprised that you suppose no going into the sea, for from those very little black spots you describe in the Map the place takes its name, there being no appearance of

Rock on the Shore, but a full description of the place you shall have when we get there. . . .

I don't love to make *mischief* but I really think you will have occasion to look a little Green when I tell you that Mr Farrer (a gentleman who is in the House) has just sent Lady Newdigate an Italian translation from the Greek of the adventures of Sappo which if she likes he begs she will take to Bognor for her amusement.

From Lady Newdigate

Ten o'Clock Friday.—It seems quite ungrateful to feel glad to Leave these good & very *Coind* friends but the thought of setting out for our Little Bognor Cabin raises our Spirits to such a pitch that we can't comport ourselves with becoming Gravity on the occasion. The Chaise with our Abigails & John are setting out as they are to hire & buy many necessary articles at Chichester which we are doubtful of getting at Bognor; & Mrs Barwell sends Rycroft with them to shew them the shops & dispose ye people to favor us. She is to go on to Bognor & they send a Carriage for her in the evening. Mrs B. lends me a Charming Pillion & a telescope. In short we have everything we want or wish for from these hospitable People. . . . I don't wonder you c^d not find our Rocks; they are to be seen only when ye Tide is out & are just what ye Maps describe, black spots that run in a Line 2 miles out to sea, & are an effectual Guard against foreign invasion; for no vessels dare come near them. . . . There are still some parts of this Noble Mansion which I have not seen & am going over this morning with Mr Barwell . . . God bless you all.

CHAPTER XII

1795

> The eldest . . . was as fine a specimen of the old English gentleman as could well have been found in those venerable days of cocked hats and pigtails. His dark eyes sparkled under projecting brows, made more prominent by bushy grizzled eyebrows; but any apprehension of severity excited by these penetrating eyes and by a somewhat aquiline nose was allayed by the good-natured lines about the mouth, which retained all its teeth and its vigour of expression in spite of sixty winters.
>
> Mr. Gilfil's Love-story.

Lady Newdigate's letters from Bognor Rocks are here continued from the last chapter. She writes on Sunday, August 23 :

Oh Dear a 2nd Letter from Arbury is gone to Stansted since we left it. Mr. Barwell sent y^c 1st to Chichester immediately & I had it ye same day, but no letter to-day & no post to-morrow. You were well however thank God, & I trust your next will be all glee on hearing that I was able to go to Portsmouth ye day after our disappointment & that I went thro' a very trying day so well & was not afterwards ye worse for it. When I reflect on ye events of that day I can scarcely believe them real. I seem as much out at sea as I am now writing at my Dining Room Window. But it has been perfectly calm & placid since we came here. Y^e Moon and Jupiter are now just opposite to me & are most beautifully reflected in ye Sea. Oh! that you could see our habitation! it is really y^e

pretyest thing you can Conceive, and ye perfect retirement we are in a pleasing contrast to ye numerous family at Stansted & almost incredible in a Place so Brimfull of Faces that one knows. Mr. & Mrs. Sheridan, the Speaker & his family (besides some others who c^d not get houses & went back to Chichester) arrived yesterday, & ye only empty house in ye Place is I hear engaged for L^d & L^{dy} Loughborough who come to-morrow; but no body visits or associates with any but their own party, so you may imagine that we have time enough upon our hands, but as far as I can judge from ye 2 Days I have been here the Life of Bognor will be a busy one. To-day has been less so than it ought & that we intended owing to Mrs. Gowan disappointing us. I sent to her yesterday for information about Church & she sent word that ye Parish Church was so small that ye Company was forced to divide & part go to the Church of Felpham, but that we sh'd get no places at all unless she 1st put us in a way. So we sat with our Cloaks on expecting the Old Lady & she never came at all. The reason was Company pour'd in so fast that she c^d not get to us till it was too late. To-morrow I think will be too short for ye demands upon it. Milly goes into the warm Bath at 8, after which we breakfast & then drive to Chichester to bespeak new springs for my Phaeton, for both have fail'd just in ye manner they have always done before, but are tyed up as they say to be perfectly safe. We also must get materials for Bathing Dresses. In short I find it will be necessary to go for almost everything we want to that place, & a more delightful road & pleasant drive it is not possible to have. I must be back by 2 to take my Warm

Bath & at 3 we dine upon roast Beef & good Potatoes & ye finest large Prawns or most excellent small Lobsters or Crabs that can be eaten. We feast upon them alternately, & always wish that we c^d send you some in a Letter. At 5 we always sally forth to walk upon ye sands or beach according as ye tide serves. To-night it was ye latter, full tide, & 2 large Ships in view tacking against ye Winds ye whole afternoon. Only think of my taking an Evening Walk ½ a mile End ways! Indeed I can hardly believe it myself. My Knee feels quite Well, but sleep does not come yet.

Augst 25th. Tuesday night ½ past 7 o'Clock.—Just come in from a Charming Drive the Moon & Jupiter lighting up ye Sea most beautifully. We work ye Dear Poneys well, they were 2 hours upon ye Sands this morning & behaved Charmingly. We quited our Carriage where ye Sands were fine & walk'd, Oh! it was delightful! They are busy as possible in this Country getting in Barley, pease and Beans, most of the wheat is in & they say the Crops are in General pretty good. I hope they will turn out so with you & that we shall eat many a good Loaf of Arbury Wheat together before ye End of ye Year. . . . The Man who supplys us here with excellent Milk & Butter is a Warwickshire man— his name Prestidge; enquires most affectionately after you and Mrs Conyers. He made Betty give him all she knew of your Life & Conversation for years back; remembers that you rode a fine spirited horse when you was Major of ye War^{re} Mil^a. He is a fine Grey headed old man & for his Love of you & Molly, Milly & I are grieved that we can't do every thing that he asks us.

He keeps Bathing Machines, but they stand at an inconvenient distance from us. . . .

Friday morning.—Two great Events in our walk last night. A lady who was siting on a Bench by Lady Pembroke got up & spoke to me as I pass'd. It was Mrs. Robinson, Lord Malmesbury's sister & at 10 just as we were moving towards bed a Message came from L^d & Lady Hood. They were to sleep at ye Hotel & depart at nine this m^g. I mounted the Dear Grey at ½ past seven & as I came up from ye sands saw Ld Hood's long Nose & scorch'd face looking out of ye Window. I turn'd my horse to speak to him when L^{dy} H. also appear'd & at ye instant Milly arrived to enquire after her Ladyship. We sat with them whilst they Breakfasted & then walked home to our own. I am glad we saw them for ye Barwells are to dine with them to-morrow. . . . I pleas'd myself with thinking that our Eyes met in ye Moon last night. Indeed it was impossible to be otherwise unless you never look'd at it for Milly and I admired her & Jupiter & their reflection in ye Sea till we were almost blind. . . .

Sunday morn^g ½ *past* 9.—Another glorious day. . . . Church is in ye afternoon at ½ past 2, but we shall be there sooner to secure places as they say some Ladies sat by the Door last Sunday & some c^d not get in at all. It is ye smallest Church I ever saw. Sir R. Hotham has built a very spacious Chapel joyning to his own house, but it is not quite finished & if they are as tedious about that as about ye Warm Bath there may be no Service in it till ye Place is out of fashion.

Monday morning.—. . . I think if you do not object

that 3 weeks is as long as I sh'd wish to stay at this place, after which I hope every step will bring me nearer dear Arbury. The kindnesses we have experienced from ye Barwell house & ye number of necessaries they have sent us makes it necessary we sh'd go that way to restore them & give them at least one day, after which our Route may be any way we please & I wish for y^r opinion upon ye subject. Poor Jessy [Mrs. Charles Parker] has written us a most pressing Letter to seduce us as far as Harefield out of our Road . . . but I will not answer her Letter till I have your thoughts. Our Weather [is] enchanting and as ye Moon after to-day w^d not serve our friends from Stansted, I rather expect them & in Consiquence sent John upon Grey for Mutton & Wine from Chichester or *Tea-chester* as both he & Betty persist in Calling it. Here he comes with our provisions. Our feast will consist of Neck of Mutton, Lamb Steaks, Cold Beef, Lobsters Prawns & Tart.

2nd Sept.—What weather we must have had & how well I must have been, out every day & almost all day ever since I left Arbury & never yet to have been in my Post Chaise, but have just order'd a p^r of horses from ye Inn & shall use it at 8 to-night for ye 1st time on an occasion that I will give you & y^r Company each 100 Guesses to find out, & after that when I tell you you will lift up your hands with surprize but without any mixture of Joy, for you will suspect as we much fear that our happy insignificance & ease will be somewhat spoilt for ye rest of our time here. Now you must know that as we were sitting quietly with our Book & Work yesterday, a Coach stop'd at our Door & the Dutchess of Devonshire was announced. She was quite shock'd to learn that we had been more than a Week in this Place. She did not know it till she saw us at Church on Sunday. She sh'd have said 'till I saw your pretty singular Equipage & enquired who it belong'd to' for I am sure she could not remember either Milly's face or mine. However all this was very Civil & after enquiring Particularly after my Brother & L^d & L^{dy} Charles etc. she told us that her Children & all ye young people ye Place affords were to meet at her Lodgings this Evening & to have a dance & she sh'd take it as a particular favor if we w^d Look in upon them. I find everybody she visits intends to do so, therefore to avoid being particular we must do ye same. We shall see assembled all ye great World of Bognor Rocks & as you are not in Parl^t & Ned's Consiquence does not extend beyond Derbyshire I hope nobody Else will honor us with their notice. . . . No company from Stansted yesterday. . . . I have made my Lame Knee *that was* a bandage so Complete that I sh'd not be afraid to dance a horn pipe with ye Duke of Devonshire if he sh'd be very importunate. . . .

From Mrs. Barton to her daughter Nelly at Arbury.

. . . Only think of our going to a Ball. How we shall equip ourselves for the occation I don't know for Barrett thinking we should have no occation for them has left all our smart things at Stansted, but you shall certainly be inform'd what appearance we make.

[The letter with the account of this party is unfortunately missing.]

Thursday 3rd Sep^t.—Our friends [Barwells] came

Loaded with good things from ye Garden which is what is most wanted here, 2 Phaetons & a post Chaise in wch were M^r & Mrs Barwell, Mrs Colbeck, Miss Gore, Mr Brown & Mr Impey. I look upon ye Gentleman's [1] Visit as a much greater honor than that of our Grand Duchess, for in regard to visits he is as immoveable as a certain Warwickshire Bart, & though he said he w^d beat up our Quarters & ye Rocks when we left Stansted both Milly & his good Little Wife were so sure he w^d not that ye Latter fearing I sh'd think it a necessary Comp^t desired Milly to assure me that he never went any where. But I never saw a Gentleman enjoy himself more, nor a whole Party more pleasant & well satisfy'd. Indeed we gave them a most excellent Dinner dress'd by Betty at a little fire about ye size of my Bed Chamber grate at Arbury,—2 Courses, a remove & desert. They stay'd with us till 7 & having a relay of horses at Chichester w^d be at home before nine. Many kind arguments were made use of to induce us to remove to Stansted & if not acceded to, that when I leave Bognor we w^d make some stay. The Warm Bath sh^d be made still more commodious & Barwell w^d engage a Boat by the Day that I may take a sail whenever I please. These proposals not being Listen'd to Y^r Angel went away saying she w^d write to you. . . . Of all ye Places I ever was in this is ye Dearest, one week's bill for my 3 horses & standing of Carriages £3. 4. 6 but you seem not to care how soon I ruin you, so God bless you and all your sweet Companions. . . .

Sunday Sep^t 6.—Thank God for a calm bright day, it puts quite another face upon our Ideas. The thunderstorm on Thursday of which we had only the skirts made such

---

[1] Mr. Barwell.

a Combustion in the Air & Sea that the Latter was quite tremendous to behold all friday & yesterday & I thought ye Wind w^d have blown us in our Little Cabin to Chichester. . . . You are very good in desiring me not to tye myself down to a Day or Week. You may be sure I shall not Loiter, having every reason that a Woman can have to prefer home to all other places. I doubt I cannot stay less than 2 days at Stansted & hard work we shall have to Combat ye many amusing schemes they have plan'd for us, but we certainly shall crush them all & proceed to Harefield a most excellent road & 2 easy days ; 2 or 3 days will not more than satisfy poor dear Jessy. When we get to St Albans our road is familiar. . . .

Tuesday ye 8th.—. . . Your friend Prestedge still raves about you & gives us ye best of Milk & Butter for your sake. He says if I mention'd ye name of Souch you w^d have remember'd him. He was at Arbury at a fishing, when Ld Denbigh was there, & saw a *Carp* taken out of your Pool that weigh'd 22lb. He must mean a Jack. . . . Your Nymphs & Graces are good Souls. To be sure the same amusements are not exactly suitable to their Age & yours but you afford a Blessed proof that when each side endeavours to meet the other's wishes, the Distance is never insurmountable. . . .

Wednesday ye 9th.—. . . To-morrow not being Bathing day we mean to take a frisk & see Worthing, 20 miles, Charming Road, ye Poneys will do it in 3½ hours. We'll take our Night Caps as there is a good Hotel in Case we sh'd meet with any agreable friend or for any reason wish to stay all night, but our plan is to set out at 8, arrive at ½ past 11, dine & see ye Lyons by 3 & return before dark, for we are aware that we have no Moon. All this depends upon ye report that John makes of ye security of the springs, they are well bound up & have never fail'd since, & I have ordered an additional band so I think we may venture safely.

Thursday.—Oh what fools we were to take fright at a few Clouds yesterday! it turn'd out most heavenly & to-day is like unto it, but nothing must stop Bathing. . . . I have no Evil but . . . want of sleep to complain of & how strange it is that sh'd not mend. . . . I try to be as patient as possible, but indeed it is at times hard to bear. Having (thank God) no pain, my *fretful* temper sometimes thinks my Complaint is less bearable. Oh I am glad Letters are come for this is a bad strain. Charming Letters that brighten ye Ideas. I wish to expunge ye few Lines above but will not. You shall have my thoughts just as they occur. We are going to drive to Chichester & here comes a Cart from Stansted loaded with fruit & Garden Stuff of all kinds, & a kind note of enquiries. I must answer it. Adieu.

Sunday ye 13th.—. . . Our Dutchess is here still, that is her Children & family, for she spends most of her time at Goodwood. Y^e Dutchess of Rutland also & her two Beautiful Boys ride about & ornament ye Place. She has generally Arthur Paget by her side. I find he succeeds his Brother in her good Graces; she seems quite proud of shewing that at 40 she has charms to attract a young man of 20. What a foolish Woman! . . .

Tuesday 15th.—. . . Here has been a 3 mast vessel, so near that with ye Telescope we could distinguish every Rope, hovering about us all morning. It is now on shore about ½ a mile off with all its Sails down. I suspect it to be a smuggler & hope now to succeed in getting you some India Hand^{ks} which hitherto I have try'd for in Vain. There are many Whisperers about & I have yielded a Little to temptation, which together with a few necessarys we were oblig'd to purchase will make our trunk which was very full before, quite overflow, so I have determined to get a Box & send by London from Stansted. So if you have any Commissions for me send them directly. I can Smuggle almost as well at Stansted or Southampton as here, but don't publish this beyond your own Circle. If you do I shall have Commissions to fill a Waggon. . . .

Stansted, Saturday [19th].—I had a charming Bath before I set out from Bognor yesterday. It revived & Cooled me & enabled me to bear the very hottest & most dusty drive I ever had in my Life. . . . We were glad to rest a Little at Chichester & arrived ourselves at Stansted just at 4. All out, driving or riding & dinner not till six. What a Change from ye sober hours we left a month ago! We expected to find the House quite full of all ye Amsterdam Hopes, M^r & Mrs Vernon etc. etc. but Nanny Ashcroft met us with a smiling Countenance & told us those 2 familys went off that morning & that there remained no additional females to ye family Party but Old Mrs Hale, Mr Rigby's sister. Men there are in plenty but of a particular Class that one sees nowhere else, & except that they fill a long Table at Meals are no annoyance. What luck we are in to escape all ye Mynheers! Our friends received us gladly & kindly. . . . I found your Letter & y^e ½ note for 50 enclosed. If you pay all demands in like proportion people will like to trade with you. I told you

£20 w^d do for me. What a Silly Man you are! ... As you are so good my Dr Soul to leave us quite to our own discretion it is just determined in Council that we set out for Harefield on Wednesday ... & eat ye most relishing Mich^s Goose that ever was roasted with you on Tuesday. ... Barwell has just sent Milly with a Ball of solid Opium weighing at least 2lb. wch he desires may be my Bed fellow to-night. That cannot hurt & he is sure it will make me sleep. I will certainly try it. I have not time to tell you of the sweet drive we had yesterday ... ye day heavenly & every yard seemed to give health & spirits yet y^r perverse wife c^d not sleep. But all will go well by & bye I doubt not. God bless you.

Harefield Lodge 7 o'Clock Thursday.—You'll like to see ye date from this place & to know that the Sisters & Poneys have perform'd Well. We left our friends at Stansted at 10 yesterday, very sorry I do believe to lose us & found dear Jessy as glad to receive us. She looks Ill but behav'd with great resolution & composure, the children all well & full of Joy ... ye Boy stout, noisy & good humour'd. I have borne my journey well, indeed ye Weather & roads were delightful but ye Dust insupportable & so deep ye sand & gravell from Farnham to Windsor that I did not think ye Poneys c^d have drawn us up ye Hills. They were 5 hours bringing us 24 miles to Windsor where I left them & ye Maids to dine & with Post Horses to ye Chaise got here at ½ pst 3. I never in my Life had a better bed than last night at ye Bush at Farnham & I really rested better than Common & feel very well but rather tired & Blind with Dust. We are drinking your health in Tea. Adieu.

CHAPTER XIII

1797

'Sir Christopher, as I understand, is going to make a clean new thing of the old Manor house both inside and out. . . .'

'But what does my lady say to 't?'

'My lady knows better than cross Sir Cristifer in what he's set his mind on,' said Mr. Bellamy. . . . 'Sir Cristifer 'll hev his own way, *that* you may tek your oath. An' i' the right on 't too. He's a gentleman born an's got the money.'—MR. GILFIL'S LOVE-STORY.

THE next batch of letters, chronicling a visit to the seaside, were written by Lady Newdigate in the summer of 1797, when she spent some weeks at Brighton. She was accompanied by her sister Mrs. Barton and the latter's daughter Nelly, a girl of seventeen at this date.

They left Arbury towards the end of June, and Lady Newdigate writes first from Daventry:

We wish all our good friends who are so anxious about us c^d know how fortunate & prosperous our 1st Days journey has been. In spite of the very worst of winter roads the day & drive has been pleasant. I never saw this Road so rutted, so heavy or so deep. It was with difficulty my poor Poneys c^d drag us to Dunchurch by half past two o'Clock. There we all got an excellent Dinner which we devour'd as we do Molly's Sunday dinners, & stay'd till half past 5 in order to follow ye Tail of a shower which we jockey'd most happily without a drop over head, but ye Road was in a Swim, Braunston Hill so heavy that I have made my hand shake with whiping my Horses, but am not at all fatigued, or is Milly, nor no Bee in her Ear.

... We have drank Tea, heard a fine Concert from ye next Room & I have been into ye town & have bought myself a Whip & my Postillion a Silver Band for his Hat. I fancy they c^d not get one at Nuneaton for it was sent with only a Cord. Now we are very Smart. . . .

Dunstable Tuesday night.—. . . Roads so deep and heavy I really never saw for such a length of way. We set out at 8 o'Clock & with difficulty reach'd Stoney Stratford at ½ past 12, Baited there 3 hours & just got to ye top of Chalk Hill as ye sun sank into his Bed. Poneys have had a hard day, but I gave them time & put in my new one for one Stage; he perform'd well & all three are eating their corn very comfortably. . . . I mean to be out before 8 to-morrow, but shall not be in town in time for ye post, but I hope you may conclude us safely landed in Piccadilly before or about 6.

Thursday 2 o'Clock 27th June 1797.—. . . Not a drop of Rain had we yesterday, but found ye Streets in Streams from a Thunder Shower there had been 2 hours before. . . . *4 o'Clock.*—Interrupted by 3 separate partys of ye Grafton family. . . . Dr. Pitcairne for Milly. . . . He recommended ye Air & Sea at Brighthelmstone. Milly told him we had thoughts of going to Bognor Rocks. He said that was by no means a good Air: so says Denman & wonders that we were not annoy'd by the stinking marshes when there. . . . They have quite decided us for Brighthelmstone which is nearer & we determine to set out on Monday. I have had ye punctual Penny who promises his orders in time, tho' I am sorry to say they go beyond your instructions, for when Rich'd & Will came in to be measured it appear'd that ye formers Livery being made for a Less Man, the Elbows were coming thro' & Will^ms was not only quite thread bare but one skirt had been torn off & patch'd on again. I thought therefore you would not disapprove of my ordering them New Liveries as well as riding Frocks; & hats they must also have. Rich^d's is very shabby indeed & Will never has had one. The Boys cap I have not bespoke, ye Sea air will tarnish it & make it unfit to go with ye new one & his Hat & Silver Band Looks very well.

Friday 2 o'Clock.—. . . At ten a Dear Letter from you. Sorry for y^r loss of Carp, but more so that you sh^d be plagued. Y^r story of progress with Towers delightful & that you are all well still better, but pray don't starve your Guests. Consider that I & my suite (horses excepted) Live free of cost till Monday. . . .

Saturday 1st July.—. . . I have just seen Fairy [Miss Cotton] & Learnt all ye ways of Brighthelmstone. She will write about a house that will just suit us & upon her recommendation I have engaged a *profess* Cook who has lived 4 y^rs with Mrs Leigh so you may expect to hear we give Dinners to ye Prince of Wales & L^dy Jersey, if they sh'd arrive whilst we stay.

Sunday night.—. . . We made our Quality visits after Church & then Drove to Hammersmith & to Kensington Palace, Mrs Cotton with Rheumatism bent double, Fairy blooming, & she gave us hints & instructions about Brighton that will be of use to us, & has order'd a person to meet us at ye Inn & inform us of all ye pleasant houses disengaged. We shall probably have Choice, for no body of the *World* thinks of going there before ye end of August & Camps there will be none near. Ned believes there is to be only one at Weymouth.

Monday mornᵍ.—. . . We can't set out to-day, Milly has business that she wᵈ be vex'd to leave undone & my brother & Nelly say we don't inconvenience them tho' I think we must.

Tuesday.—We cᵈ not have gone yesterday if we had intended it for about yᵉ time we sh'd have set out Nelly Barton was seized with such an odd sleepyness & sickness & head Ach that we were forced to put her to Bed. . . . We thought it expedient to send for Cotton, Evans's son-in-law & successor, a very sensible honest man. . . . He hopes she will be able to move in a day or two, but it would be very hazardous in her present state. He does not apprehend Meazles which Milly fear'd but a violent attack of yᵉ Complaint that has been so long in fashion. . . . My Brother & Nelly are so very kind & make so light of yᵉ inconvenience we must put them to by breaking their plans which were arranged for leaving town on Thursday that we have every possible Consolation.

Thursday 6th July.—Thank God our minds are perfectly Easy for Nelly B's safety. The throat is almost Well but yᵉ Day is bad & she is not in a state to run hazzards. To mend yᵉ Matter my man Richᵈ has been in Bed with a fever & taking repeated doses of James since Noon yesterday. . . . I found out by accident he was Ill for yᵉ foolish fellow wish'd to Conceal it wᶜʰ might have cost him his Life & wᵈ have been a great distress to me. As it is he need not keep me in town if Nelly is able to go to-morrow of which I make no doubt, as I can leave him another day to recover, & he may be down by yᵉ stage to meet me. . . . I am quite well, but a Letter from Wandon [1]

---

[1] The home of Lady Charles FitzRoy, *née* Mundy.

has fill'd us with anxiety. Ld Charles is very Ill of a Billious fever. The Apothecary certainly fears it to be of a putrid tendency as he has order'd him Bark & two bottles of Wine a day. They have sent for Doct^r Carr from Northampton but he was not arrived when ye post came away. Ned will wait for to-morrow's post & if he finds that Carr cannot go to him, he immediately sets out & Carrys down Doctor Hallifax. We have had 3 or 4 sets of Fitzroys this morning making anxious enquiries after Ld Charles. It will be a satisfaction to us to see to-morrow's acc^t before we set out. It is dreadful to think how long these sort of Complaints have prevail'd in town & country. Thank God all that are very near & dear to us have come off well.

Friday 7th July, one o'Clock.—. . . We are habited, pack'd & I hope shall actually re-commence our Journey between 3 & 4 o'Clock. Nelly is quite free from Fever & Sore Throat but I never saw any thing so Low & languid. . . .

We are to Dine at 2 o'Clock & my Sister, Frederick & Henry will be so Vulgar as to eat with us at that Uncouth hour. My Brother alass! is just setting out with Doct^r Hallifax for Wandon. Carr has been over, dis-approves of what has been done before & put Ld Chas into a Course of James's Powders. As his extensive business will not allow him to stay with him the Duke will not be satisfy'd without Hallifax goes down & stays. My Bro^r has seen him & settled their Journey at 2 o'Clock. He says from ye Acc^{ts} the fever is certainly of a bad kind but no allarming symtoms are mention'd. I am glad my Bro. goes down for poor Fanny has no body with her & is in a state of anxiety which must be hurtful in her situation. . . . I have never found Room or time for a word of Politicks, but there is no news but what you have in ye papers. I think everybody that are friends to their Country are in good Spirits & think that ye late efforts of the Mischievous have done infinite good & that the Navy will be in greater subordination & be better regulated than it has ever been. The night before last Ned (y^u younger) saw a french Gentleman turn'd out of ye Play house for saying in a low Voice 'Vive la Republic.' An Officer with one Arm in a Sling took notice of it and said if he was able he w^d *turn him out* & he was hustled out of the Box & made ye best of his way out of ye house. The publick Enthusiasm in favor of English tars is for ye present quite gone. Ned says that passages in ye Theater that w^d till now have set ye house in a Roar of Applause is now rec^d with Coldness. I hope they will be Ambitious to regain their Popularity.

Brighthelmstone, Sunday July ye 9th.—I must break through ye order of my Journal & introduce you at once to ye neatest, pleasantest & most Comfortable House that you can form an Idea of, & assure you that we are all well & had a delightful pleasant journey. . . . Y^e post was gone before we got to Reigate, a Clean, good Inn & good Beds. As our two Invalids seem'd a Little tired I thought it best not to hurry them out in ye Morning, so order'd Rich^d to wait & attend Mrs. Barton's Chaise at her own time. But as it was expedient that we sh'd get as early as possible to Brighton I called Kerry before 6 o'Clock, order'd Willm & ye Phaeton, got a dish of Coffee & set out with my Maid by my side at 7. . . . I had y^e

pleasantest of drives 19 miles to Cuckfield where I order'd a good dinner which was ready to come upon Table when ye Posters arrived. By the time we had swallowed it Poneys had had a long Bait & we proceeded prosperously & pleasantly to the Great Castle Inn at this Place, sent immediately for our Letters & for Fairy's friend who has many houses of her own to let which in Course she carry'd us to first . . . but she very handsomely told us of 7 or 8 others & advised us to see them before we fixt. One of the number is ye one we are in wch has this advantage over all we have seen that every Bed Chamber is airy & has a view of ye Sea. . . . I am to give 6 guineas per week as I take it by ye week only. It is ye last house upon ye Steyne near ye Sea. I was sorry not to take Mrs. Howell's house, she behaved so handsomely. Nelly [Mundy] w^d I am sure have done it & have put herself into a Close back Room, don't you think she w^d? . . . By 8 o'Clock we were comfortably settled in our House. The Cook seems an orderly sensible Woman. She is to market, Cook & Clean ye house, our own Maids helping to make Beds & sweep our Rooms, so that I hope we shall want no extra helper *except* when we *give dinners to ye P. of W^s* whose pavillion we see from our windows, & we also see at this instant a fine *Bed of Tulips* upon ye Steyne, Bonnets, Blue & Yellow etc. but they are people that *no body knows*. We took our Walk before ye world came out & are now going to afternoon Church. . . . The air feels soft & balsamic & we all fancy ourselves ye better for it already. . . . Thank God we have a better acc^t of Ld Charles than we expected. I dare say you have it also from Nelly. . . . How Charmingly you get on with your *Turrets*! I was so ignorant as not to know that yᵉ Arrow was a New Idea for a Vane. I think it a very good one. I can believe that you all rejoyce at Denman's [her doctor's] good report, but am sorry dear Sally was glad over much. Neither Joy nor Sorrow in the extreme is good for her : tell her to write to me & tell me how she does & whether my recipe continues to agree. . . .

Monday yᶠ 10ᵗʰ.—More heavenly weather cannot be wish'd. I hope you have just such & I intended that you sh'd begin to mow last Saturday, but am afraid you did not. We have had two Hours drive upon the Downs. The day was made on purpose for us, no Sun whilst we were out, a Gentle Soft Breeze from yᵉ Sea of which we had a fine View & the Drive all upon fine Turf. I find it is the fashion to go a dusty Road in an Evening by yᵉ side of the Cliff, perhaps in Consideration for yᵉ Horses, but I think my Poneys will be able to draw me up yᵉ Hills twice a day. . . . We saw a number of Equipages upon yᵉ Downs & many drive past our house but I know not a Name they belong to. . . . I think you will like to know *how to think* of us through yᵉ Day so I will give you our General plan. Rise at 7, Bathe or Walk from eight to nine, then Breakfast; from ten till 12 or one drive upon yᵉ Downs; sit in our Bow Windows to yᵉ Sea till ½ past 3, then Dine, drink Tea at Six, drive again till near 8 & then Lounge upon yᵉ Beach or Steyne till 9 when we Sup & go to Bed at ½ pˢᵗ ten. These are yᵉ rules we have laid down & I don't think it will be in yᵉ P. of W—ses power when he comes to alter them. . . . We are hungry all day Long & there is tempting fruit which you know I cannot withstand though I give 1s. 6d. a pottle for strawberries & as much for a pound of Cherries. The fish is excellent but I daresay too dear; we gave 1s. 6d. for a pair of fine soles yesterday & 1s. 3d. for 4 fine Whitings to-day. At Bognor we seldom got any fish at all. You will Judge by the subject I write upon that I now am hungry. Indeed I am, & shall play my part with an excellent dinner viz. Fish, Roast Mutton, Cold Beef, Sallad, potatoes, Tart, Cheese & a Desert. Brava, you will say; I am sure you do not give your guests a better Dinner *except* that ye Strawberries come from Swanland. Keep yourself well & happy my Dear Life & I shall Lay in such a stock of health here that you will think me too robust & riotous when I return.

Tuesday 11th.—Very good Letter from Arbury thank God, but I am afraid for Lord Charles & very sorry for all that belong to him. Nelly too is hurry'd down to Wandon & must disappoint poor Jessy. She also disappoints Milly but not me, for I foresaw ye impossibility of her coming down here. But Milly thought as the Fitzroys must now give up their Shipley visit that she might be tempted down. But it is only sickness or distress that can draw Nelly & with those Cords I hope we shall have nothing to do. . . . I found out Mrs. Ch^s Drummond immediately when I look'd in ye Book of ye right Bookseller. We ignorant People went & subscribed to ye one that was in fashion 10 or 12 years ago & who has now only the great or rich that subscribe to both. I am glad my ignorance has procured me such distinction for ye Civil Man has lent me a Telescope for ye time I stay. The Rooms were lighted up on Sunday, but as nobody went to them ye candles were put out & will not be open'd again till ye Races, which with Sorrow I learn are to Commence ye 25th & last 3 days. Nelly B. enjoys the thought of ye Bustle; there will be ye P. of W.'s Band playing twice a day upon ye Steyne & at ye Balls. She flatters herself she shall at least get to one, but I don't know how that will be. I rather think we shall all make an excursion to Worthing or perhaps to Stansted for ye 3 days of the races. . . . So much for *you*; now for Sally. Love etc. . . . Giving dinners to 9, what Extravagance! We eat up everything we can get ourselves & have nothing for strangers.

Thursday.—I have not your Letters till ye 4th day. There you have ye advantage. Y^rs of Monday night just arrived. Nasty Astley Wake to take away your Workmen when they sh'd have occupy'd you tenfold, that you might not regret ye want of post that day. . . . A most Convenient and Chearful house we have got, but it has a defect which ye gloomyness of the Day we arrived made us not observe viz. that it fronts to ye West & is dreadfully hot in a sunshiny afternoon of which we have as yet had but 2. . . . We are going to see ye prince's Pavillion which is not shewn after his arrival, then for a Drive & ride upon ye Downs. . . . We air'd last night along the Cliff for the 1st time. I felt afraid to venture not knowing that as far as ye Road is near the Cliff which is about 3 miles, there is a strong post & Rail all ye Way. If not it w^d be tremendous indeed for ye Rock is quite perpendicular & from 50 to 200 feet high & ye Road sometimes not ye breadth of a Carriage from ye Edge. We saw a Fleet of near thirty Sail of Large Ships going towards

Portsmouth, it was delightfully pleasant. I think ye Company have *taste* to make that ye fashionable Evening Drive & we profit by their want of *sense*, for a long String of Carriages met us about a Mile from hence at eight o'Clock as we were coming home & we had ye Cliff to ourselves. . . .

Friday.— . . . I have had a very Tepid Bath this morning which has refresh'd me & made me feel comfortable after ye hottest night I ever felt in England. . . . Indeed we were all so overcome with ye heat of our Lodging yesterday & heard such an Acc^t of Coolness & Comfort from Mrs. Hale who is just removed from our neighbourhood to the Cliff that we determined to seek for a house there, & after our Evening Drive which we shorten'd for that Purpose went into every house unlet on ye Cliff & Marine Parade, in number 4 only, but fortunately one of them, the very house I think we sh'd have made Choice of if it had been at Liberty. It is quite to my taste for from ye Parlour, Drawing Room & my Bed Chamber nothing to be seen but Sea, aspect south. Milly's & Nelly's Bed Chamber east, looking over a Garden with side view of ye Sea & under them a small parlour to which we can retire if ye South aspect sh'd ever be too hot, which I think it never can be in such an elivated & airy situation. I was afraid Nell w^d have regretted the loss of this Gay Scene, but she seems as much pleased to remove as her Mother & Aunt. So to-morrow evening our week being up we become inhabitants of No. 15 Marine Parade. . . . Nelly & I are going to swallow a fine fresh Breeze upon ye Downs with Barret upon a new Poney to try for her mistress. . . .

New Poney quite a beast, we must seek further. We found ye Downs cap'd with a Cold fog so made ye best of our way down into ye Sunshine wch is tempered by a fine Breeze from ye Sea & till about 4 o'Clock nothing can be pleasanter than our present house, I mean in point of temperature, for I must always prefer a View of ye Unbounded Ocean to Red Coats & White Gowns, tho' here indeed we have a mixture of both. . . .

Marine Parade Sunday 16*th.*—Now I hope we are settled till we Leave this place. . . . We have a pretty good pull from ye Steyne to our abode which will keep us in good breath, the Baths, Librarys etc. etc. are all in that quarter. . . . Milly discovered a Fleet of 21 Sail as she lay in Bed this morning, but they are so far off that our Telescope has not power to shew us ye Colors they Carry, but we see their masts & sails very distinctly & last night a pleasure boat about a Mile & ½ distant. I could almost have *distinguish'd* ye faces of the Company on board, I don't say *known.* for I literally do not know ye face of Man or Woman in ye place except Mrs C. Drummond. . . .

Your Drawing gives me no Idea what Brighthelmstone now is. Indeed I have seen nothing yet of the part you have drawn. I am told that ye Steyne & everything beyond the Old Town has been built within ye last 30 years. I will walk all over ye place & give you ye best Map I can of it. Y^e White Cliff you speak of begins from ye Steyne by a gradual assent & where we are is about 60 feet high. I have no doubt from y^e great Bites that y^e Sea takes from it from time to time, that all these sweet Houses will in a few years share y^e fate of y^e old town you describe, tho' we have a Broad Road & Little Court between us & the Cliff thus. . . .

I have made you believe we are y^e highest part of y^e Cliff & y^e last house, but there are houses ½ a mile beyond us & much higher situation. . . .

From Mrs. Barton to Sir Roger

Brighton July ye 17th. . . . I hope you have heard ye good account from Wandon, Lord Charles quite out of danger & recovering fast so I fancy you will soon see the *Great* Nelly at Arbury; but I must Leave room for Lady N. to add her few lines so adieu. . . .

From Lady Newdigate

Milly has told so good & true a tale that I think I cannot mend it; her sleeping last night through ye Storm was beyond belief & must be ye effects of 3 or 4 sleepless nights with head ach caused by ye heat of our 1st house. I am not usually afraid of thunder but it was so loud of that Cracking kind & ye Gusts of Wind so violent that I expected ye house or at least Chimneys to fall every instant & ye Lightning so vivid & Constant thro' our Venetian blinds & thin Curtains, for we have not a Shutter in ye house, that it is wonderful to me that they escaped being on fire. I own I lay in a great fright not daring to encounter ye Lightning thro' ye Staircase window wch appeared worse from the wind down my chimney having put out my rush light. . . .

Tuesday 10 *o'Clock*.—. . . . Last night the dust being laid on ye Roads & ye Wind & Waves not enough appeased since ye Storm of ye night before to make ye Cliff or Downs pleasant . . . we drove to Lord Pelham's, 4 Miles from hence. . . . As the family is not there ye Woman at ye Lodge made no scruple of letting us into ye park & told us we might go out at ye Lodge at ye other End & find a track over ye Downs to Brighton. . . . Nelly canter'd by the side of us 3 Miles thro' a most Beautiful Tumbled & well planted Park & over ye Downs delightful. . . . I wish I c^d give your Rheumatic wrists & arms a few soakings in these Charming Baths. I am sure it w^d Cure you. Old Fairy says she has not known such Comfort these 20 years as since she has Bathed a few weeks every summer in warm Sea water.

Thursday ye 20th.—. . . This morning it rains & has oblidged me to have a Chair to & from ye Bath, ye 1st time, except in London that I have got into a Cover Conveyance since I left Arbury. . . . Mr Barwell complimented me & Nelly upon our good looks. If he has good acc^ts of his Boy & of Mrs B.'s spirits he will stay 2 days of ye Race in his way Back. . . . We shall leave ye length of our stay to be determined by you & now I'll tell you my Ideas. When we leave the seaside ... we need make only 2 days from hence to Harefield ; to Ryegate y^c 1st day ; from thence 21 miles to *Mundy's Hotel* Piccadilly where we can have a dinner from ye Tavern & if you wish it, see Denman ... but all this, likewise whether we stay one day or more with Jessy & *when* we leave Brighton shall be subject to your direction. Denman & Pitcairne both said that under a month no great benefit was to be expected. That will bring us to Saturday ye 5th of August. Speak your Mind, I am sure it is that of myself & Dear Companions. ...

Friday ye 21st.—. ... I am glad you understand my Drawing. If you have patience & will give me time to execute my great design, you shall know all that you wish to know. The old Town is all to ye West of ye Steyne & the Church upon a hill behind it. I have got a Map of ye Place in '88 & am adding all that is done since ; also a ground Plan & Elevation of our House is in hand, but what with watching ye Sea, Driving, walking & writing, I get but little Time for other Works. I rejoyce that Burgess & Sarah are well again, you have shew'd great Medical Skill, I hope for the last time it will be wanted. ... I have not answered you about ye Steyne, will describe it on ye next Leaf, but that must be after Dinner, for we are in a hurry to eat Whitings & Mutton.

Y^e fishing boats are out to-day. Only 2 have ventured since Sunday & we watch'd them coming in with Terror ; they kept throwing out ye Water on both sides as far off as we c^d distinguish & were 2 hours battling ye Waves not 20 y^{ds} from ye Shore.

Saturday 22nd.—What a Change in our prospect! Instead of great Foaming Billows that made one dread to see a Ship or Boat at Sea we have now a Sheet of Glass before us that w^d not hurt a fly. . . . This place fills very fast, but with whom I know not. Milly hears that ye house we have left is taken for *The* Mrs Pitt, but I want faith & don't Care. There seems to me to be more Children than ever were assembled in any place before, I suppose from ye Idea that ye Air is so pure; & indeed I do think there is something uncommonly mild & balsamic in it. . . . We had a new & delightful airing last night up ye hill by Brighton Church on a fine Road over ye Downs. About 5 miles & ½ is what is call'd ye Devil's Gap, & is a Lyon that everybody goes to see. I thought we were too late to go so far & mean to attack it in a Morning. Here comes Milly enchanted with her Ride, y^e horse, y^e Day & y^e prospect all delightful. She bids me thank you for your Letter, finish mine & get some Cloaths upon my Back for I am writing in my Bed Gown & it is near our Dinner time. Distribute Love throughout y^r Empire. Adieu.

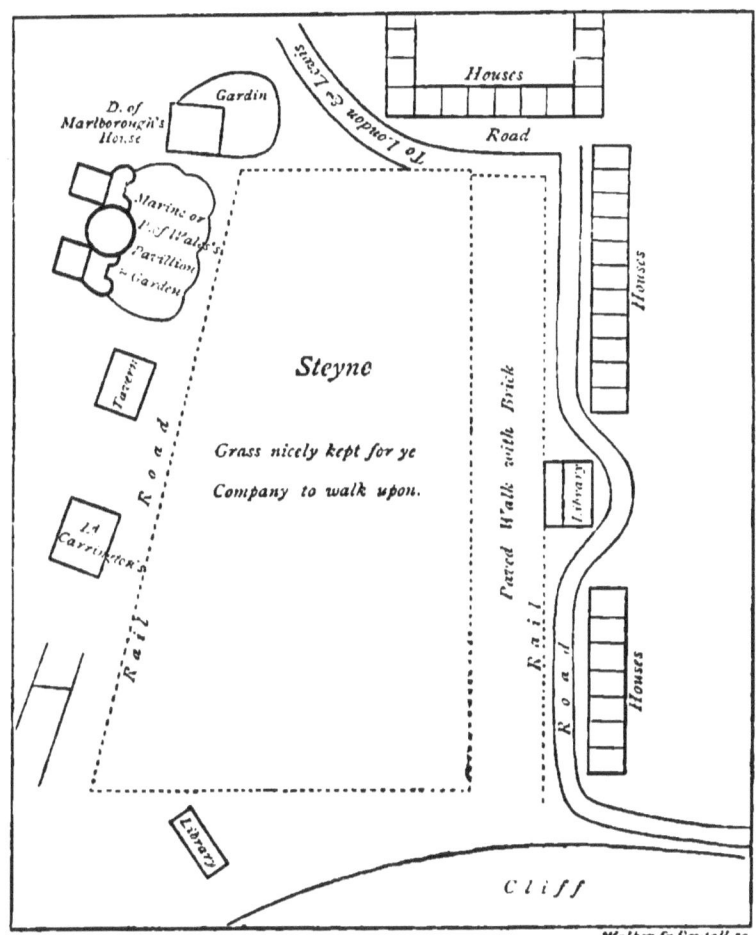

CHAPTER XIV

1797

> Last of all came a couple whom the villagers eyed yet more eagerly than the bride and bridegroom. A fine old gentleman, who looked round with keen glances that cowed the conscious scapegraces among them, and a stately lady in blue-and-white silk robes, who must surely be like Queen Charlotte.—Mr. GILFIL'S LOVE-STORY.

LADY NEWDIGATE continues her letters from Brighton, the next being dated Sunday, July 23.

A mighty good day with us. . . . My Companions are in high health & spirits. Milly has slept as she did in the thunderstorm & feels well & hungry, & myself & Nelly ditto. . . . Many Great arrivals yesterday. Amongst ye rest L^d and L^{dy} Jersey & family: they have a House upon ye Steyne just opposite to the Pavillion, ye owner of wch is expected to-night. They will gain their Ends by impudent perseverance, for nobody seems to think there will be any Bustle made this Year. *We* shall receive them Civilly. . . . Oh how I like a Letter that begins in Verse. I cannot like Audrey thank ye Gods that they have not made me Poetical.

Monday 24th.—Nasty Monday brings me no Letter & it is pay day so I have my Week's acc^{ts} to settle. It is necessary to know how fast money goes that I may be able to tell you how many hundreds or thousands will redeem me from this Place. Gambling season does not begin till to-morrow, so the great Charge at present is Eating & drinking, I assure you we live well & upon great delicacies. I have marketed myself this morning, given 3^s for a Turbot & 2. 6^d for Cherries & Strawberries, all Luxuries these, nothing towards feeding ye family you see. . . . Just come out of my Pickling Tub. . . . Prince expected every minute. Duke of Bedford, Sir John Lade & many of ye Turf arrived. I have promised to take Nell to ye Course one day, *not in my Phaeton*, but to have a pair of horses to Milly's Chaise & my two serv^{ts} to attend me & to go with her one Night to ye Ball, but we have not yet determined which it shall be. I don't think poor Milly can determine whether she can stand ye meeting of so many of B. . .'s old Croneys who possibly may recollect her. I shall not press her upon ye subject. I will go with Nelly who will be perfectly in Cog. with me, for I have not seen a Man yet that I know well enough to Curtsey to. . . .

Tuesday ye 25th.—I am a Solitary Being, have walk'd upon ye Cliff & Steyne & have sat an hour upon a Marine Stool which I have treated myself with, amongst nurses & children upon ye Beech till ye waves wash'd my feet & I removed several times out of their reach. Very delightful indeed! I envy'd not the Mad World upon ye Race ground. Thither my Companions are gone. You need not preach to me care of ye Hills. I do encounter the best of them in my own Dear Carriage, but found my Courage quite unequal to ye task of going upon sidelong Hills among a number of Carriages with Hack Horses & Postillions. So Milly is gone with her Girl & I have sent Rich^d & Willm upon ye Galloways to attend them &

o

Charles is my Porter & Guard. When I open'd your Letter c⁴ not recollect what I had said to put you into such a puff. It was only that I complain'd of your not writing yᵉ days it was almost impossible you sh'd write so you may guess what you have to expect. You write very sweetly & kindly about our stay here & Milly is full of Gratitude for it. Her Spirits are so improvĕd within these few days that I do really hope y' Completion of our Month will find her very essentially benefited. She did not seem this Morning to have the feelings I suspected about going to yᵉ Race, & yesterday's journal will speak for yᵉ health & Spirits of yᵉ Trio, but as I owe M. L.[1] a very kind & acceptable note the History of our Riots & disgrace shall be inscribed to her.

To Miss Millicent Ludford

MY DEAR MILLY,—Your tender Care of my Husband Convinces me that you are my very true friend & therefore I shall depend upon you to soften yᵉ following relation, & moderate yᵉ laugh it will raise against us as much as you can. I told Sir R. I had promised Nelly one Ball at yᵉ Race, so it behoved us to enquire wᶜʰ was likely to be y' best. One & all declared that for yᵉ 2 last years yᵉ Day before y' Race all the Great Company came to yᵉ Ball, & that it was more Brilliant & agreable that Night than any other during yᵉ Whole Season. Then say we 'Why sh'd not *we* partake of yᵉ best?' Miss Grosvenor who is our Neighbor & happen'd to call upon us just then, agree'd to go with us, so bonnets were taken off, Turbans etc. adjusted & at ½ pˢᵗ 9, yᵉ Genteel Hour,

[1] Millicent Ludford, daughter of Sir Roger's sister Juliana.

we repair'd to ye Ball Room which is truly magnificent indeed. It was gaily Lighted up & the Master of y^c Ceremonies walking about in it. Not another Soul. He observed to us that he never knew y^c Company come so late, but that there certainly w^d be a great deal presently. . . .

The next sheet has been torn off and is unfortunately missing. Evidently they had chosen the wrong night and nobody came at all.

From Lady Newdigate to Sir Roger

Wednesday 26th.—Now I feel remorse that my Nonsense sh'd make you send to Cov^{try} on a busy day, but your inconvenience is past & ye pleasure to me just in full force. . . . Nell was so pleased with ye Race Ground yesterday that it occupy'd & amused ye Mother & prevented unpleasant thoughts. She told me she had seen several of y^r sporting tribe that used to be Weeks at a time at Harling, but she took care not to be seen by them & they were not Men that went to Balls so sh'd run no further Chance of meeting them. P. of W. was upon ye field on horseback & always by Lady J.'s Coach when ye horses were not running. She has never appear'd except in her Carriage & nobody visits her or seems to make any fuss about her. Our Ladys Maids hear that she & her Daughters walk upon ye Steyne at hours when nobody else does & that yesterday ye Mob hiss'd her as she stood at her Window, which faces the Pavillion. We went down to ye Steyne last Night at y^c Genteel hour which is 9 o'Clock to see ye Illuminations at ye Booksellers in honour of ye Prince's arrival & to hear his Band of Musick wch played delightfully & is to play from 8 till 10 every Night. Y^e Scene was comical & pretty, very like Vauxhall, only without Trees; ye Company still more mixt. We heard that ye Duchess of Marlborough & numbers more of ye very great were there, but except just about ye Illuminations it was too dark to distinguish anybody's face. One thing pleased me which was that as soon as '*Long live the Prince*' appear'd in shining Lamps ye Mobility made ye Band strike up 'God save the King' & w^d not let them change ye tune till even *I* was tired of it. 2 or 3 turns satisfy'd us & we came home to our Boil'd Artichokes at ½ p^st 9. The Company stay'd upon ye Steyne till ½ p^st 10 & are now all gone upon ye Course. We set out as usual with Phaeton & Poney at Eleven to take a quiet airing but found it so hot we c^d not bear it. So if we do not go to ye Ball which depends upon ye report we hear, we shall take a long Drive in ye Evening. Nelly is such a reasonable pleasant Creature that I sh'd be sorry not to give her as much amusement as is good for her. She enjoys everything but seems just as happy when at home with us. I have heard of some arrivals that I must visit, Lady Evelyn, Mrs. Pigou & one or 2 more, most of them Birds of Passage come only for ye Race, but our acquaintance may increase a Little without oppressing us. Old Middleton comes to-morrow; she will be worth all ye rest to me.

And so Nelly [Mundy] is detain'd at Wandon on poor Fanny's Acc^t. She has caught ye fever of Ld Charles, very slightly Nelly assures me, but in her Situation it must be allarming & one cannot help thinking it possible that Nelly may not entirely escape, tho' she boasts much of the precautions she has taken. I shall be glad to have her safe in ye North, but she certainly cannot leave Fanny till she is as well as her present state will admit of. . . . How you will make Hay to-day if you have such weather at Arbury ! . . .

Thursday 27th.—What c^d be ye reason that you had no Letter from Nelly [Mundy] to say that L^{dy} Charles's Illness detain'd her. She c^d not have omitted writing as she knew you were expecting her. Such suspence is very uncomfortable, but it has long been over I hope & by this time the cause nearly so also, but I always think that accidental Illnesses are doubly to be dreaded in Poor Fanny's situation.

Journal continued from ye short & hot drive of yesterday. It left us no inclination to stir till evening when a Charming Breeze arose which tempted me into my Phaeton & Nell to mount her horse. As we had before determin'd to try our Luck again at ye Ball, Milly chose to sit quiet. We had a most refreshing airing till 8 o'Clock, Drank our Tea, dress'd & to ye Ball at ½ past nine. It was in truth a very shabby one for a Race Ball, not 100 people in all, but Nelly got a good Dance. The Prince of Wales just walk'd round ye Room & spoke to a few Ladies, & Milly & I saw some old acquaintances that we had not seen for some years who were very glad to see us, so it answer'd well to all ye Party & we are none of us the worse for it. We have been this morning to call upon Lady Evelyn, who upon hearing that we were to pass thro' London strongly recommended to us ye Darkyn [Dorking] Road & kindly press'd us to make an Inn of their House at Wootton. This was enforced by Sir Frederick who urged that it w^d divide our Journey much better. They are 36 miles from London. I don't love Visits on a Journey, but it is flattering & pleasant to find Warmth in very old friends, & poor Milly who before she went to India, lived a great deal with them, feels their kind remembrance quite a Cordial . . . tell me your wishes truly & I will be very obedient. . . . Our maids are walk'd to the Course; we are going to dine upon Pigeon & Cold Mutton, take a drive from six to 8 & then if we are not too Lazy hear ye Musick for ½ an hour on ye Steyne. I am not able to get at ye Etymology of that word. Everybody answers that they have ask'd ye same Question without success, but I'll go & talk to ye two Booksellers, one of them is very intelligent.

Friday 28*th*.—Oh! this is Lovely Weather indeed. If you have ye same, Mowers cannot keep pace with you & you will have done your hay in a *trice*. What does that word come from? I can make nothing of Steyne. There is a town not far off called Steyning. Mrs Middleton arrived yesterday . . . she will eat Mutton with us at ½ past 3. . . . Nell is gone with a Lame Lady in her Post Chaise to see ye Race from an opposite hill. The P. of W. being so rich that he can pay no Bills gives a Plate to-day. Otherwise ye Race w^d have ended yesterday. I am told that Lady Jersey was with all her beautiful Children at ye fireworks ye other night, not amongst ye Great but seated on a bench amongst the Vulgar, who made 2 attempts to Hiss her, but were not joyn'd by Townspeople & Company as last year. They will undoubtedly let her stay but she lives for ye P. alone, for nobody, a few young Men excepted, go to her house or are seen with her. . . . No Barwell at y^c Race. Mr Shakspeare left him at Winchelsea with a friend who had been much hurt by an over turn in a Curricle & y^c good natured Barwell c^d not resolve to leave him. . . . Here comes our Old Friend [Mrs. Middleton] . . . she was much overcome with heat & fatigue yesterday, but old Sir James Nappier of 82, who she travell'd down with, in order to take care of him, walk'd to her home before 8 o'Clock this morn^g intending to Breakfast with her. He call'd again at 9 but not finding her up, said he sh'd walk home & breakfast by himself. He was a great friend of Old Middleton & in some profession but I know not what.

Dear Nelly's words [from Wandon] are a Little dark indeed & tell me that her mind was in a very anxious state & that she c^d not determine what she sh'd do, nor what she wish'd to do, unwilling to give unnecessary allarm, yet herself believing Fanny to be more unwell than mearly her situation w^d acc^t for. . . .

Mrs Middleton insists that I send her kindest love to you & says that it does her heart good to hear you are so Well.

Sunday 30th.—You directed the Letter I have to-day with such a Shaking Hand & so Ill, without Spectacles I suppose, that I was half frightened, but thank God your Letter wears the Marks of a Steady Head, Heart & Hand & your Nymphs speak well of you, so I am happy, but how without sea Breezes was it possible to exist on friday & Saturday? Milly, & some Indian friends that are here, say they never felt such weather but in Calcutta.

I have never felt ye Downs too hot for my open Carriage till yesterday, when I was forced to put up ye Head to shade me from ye Sun & came home quite sick. We did not attempt to stir again till eight o'Clock, when we walk'd to ye Steyne & were lucky enough to find a Vacant Bench under ye Booksellers awning. There we sat, heard ye Musick & saw ye Company pass & repass, but who they were we knew not tho' ye pretty half Moon shone Bright & made a Line of Light over ye Sea, as upon ye Hall Pool which methought you were all admiring at that instant from ye Library Window. Ye Contrast between ye two scenes amused my imagination more than that of ye Grandees that were passing in Cog. At Nine we walk'd up ye Cliff to our suppers which we c^d not eat for Heat; not a breath of air even in our Temple of ye Winds & ye Night so Sultry there was no sleeping till a most violent hail storm with very moderate thunder & Lightning at 5 this morning cool'd ye Air a Little. But when I walk'd down to my Bath at 8 o'Clock I thought ye day promised to be as hot as yesterday. I waited ½ an hour for my Bath for ye Hail in ye Night had broken every Sky Light & made ye Sea water in ye Cistern unfit for use by the tiles & dirt it had brought from ye buildings. The Bath woman told me that square pieces of Ice were found that came through ye window ¾ of an Inch in size. We had one pane broke in our Dining Room & Mrs Drake upon ye Steyne had eleven. We all feel Languid to-day but otherwise well. . . . I have heard a fine Extempore Sermon evidently preached at ye P. of W. but he was not there to hear it. Poor Fanny has been very ill indeed. I do not feel very easy about her. Adieu.

Monday 31st.—. . . 5 o'Clock. Old Fairy call'd just as we were sitting down to a dinner of Cold Lamb & Sallad & Currant Tart. She sociably partook of it & I have told her that y^c like Chear may be found at ½ past 3 whenever she pleases. I have talk'd to her about my difficulties. You will suppose she advises me to stay another Week. Indeed she seems seriously to think it may be of great Consiquence to Milly. . . . I cannot repeat my old friend's arguments but you w^d with me think them weighty though they equally oppose our inclinations. . . . Well! if I must stay another week will turn my thoughts to ye benefits that will attend it *as I hope*; 1st Milly's further amendment; 2^{ndly} my own, for tho' really I do not seem to want it, am certain that both ye air & Bathing agree with me; 3^{rdly} my sick horse may recover & by that time be able to perform ye Journey with me, which there seems to be but little Chance of so soon as Saturday next. Oh dear! all our Letters will be at cross purposes for ye next five days. . . .

I have made a sort of vague calculation on money matters & find that not less than 60 or 70£ *more than I have* will bring me scot free to Arbury. Adieu. You won't like this Letter more than I do.

Tuesday ye 1st.—Oh, you Dear Dear Soul, you have releaved & comforted our Minds by y^r 2 Letters to-Day! . . . You propose us to stay just to ye Day I mention'd in my Letter yesterday which is such a Cordial to poor Milly as you can hardly conceive. . . . Our only difficulty now is with ye people of our Lodgings who have let their house from Monday ye 7th. They cannot turn us out I believe, but ye man has been to Bully me in hopes I suppose to make me pay a Little more, thinking that I have no Gentleman belonging to me, but he is mistaken. Milly went immediately to Old Middleton & found with her Mr Bowen ye nephew of Sir James Nappier, who very politely undertook our Cause, has been with ye Lady who took ye house for her friend & who promises to let me know by to-morrow night whether she will delay her coming till Saturday sen-night. If she will not, Mr Bowen advises me to quit ye house or I may be persecuted by the Man for ye rent of ye month, ye Lady has taken it for. We have so Little to remove & there are plenty of houses, so it is not worth a squabble. . . . In my Letter I cheated Sir J. Nappier of 3 years. He is turn'd 85, lost one Eye 40 y^{rs} ago, but will walk alone upon this Cliff where Gigs & flying Phaetons etc. etc. are passing every ins^t. He is moving his Lodgings because he c^d not see ye Sea.

I don't like ye acc^t from Wandon & suspect that Milly will be oblidg'd to go there instead of coming with me to Arbury. My Horse is much better to-day and Willm makes no doubt but he will get well.

Do ask of your female Croneys if they have any wants in ye Muslin way. Nothing else is worn in gowns by any Rank of people, but I don't know that I can get them cheaper here, but great Choice there is, very beautiful & real India.

Wednesday 2nd.—. . . Our Landlord I am sure is a Jacobin. I will have no more parly with him, but if the Lady is unwilling to delay her coming, we will remove for a Week, provided we can find a place to remove to, but every house seems to be taken & yet there are very few that we know even by sight & all complain that there is nobody to associate with. Y^c Princes party & Citizens make ye only figure. I think we shall be sorry not to move, for after y^c nasty man had hurry'd our spirits & made us nervous ye Violent Storm of Wind that Blew all yesterday & still continues, has made us rather dislike this very exposed situation which in Calm Weather is very delightful, but if both Winds & Jacobins roar at us we shall seek shelter in ye Peaceful scenes of Arbury sooner than we talk of unless we can settle ourselves for another week with very little Trouble. . . . Old Mid. is well & in spirits. She takes it very kindly that you wish her to Come to Arbury, but she says she's too Old for such Journeys. Indeed she is not so able as *some* who make ye same excuse. . . .

Thursday 3rd.—. . . In the Hurricane last night, when people c^d hardly stand upon their Legs upon this Cliff arrived at ye next Door a smart sociable with 4 beautiful Bay horses & smart postillions, an Old Gen^m & Lady with 2 young Ladies within, follow'd by a Coach with Domesticks drawn by Post horses. We watch'd & pity'd them in many fruitless attempts they made before they c^d get out of ye Carriage into ye house. At Supper I heard their Names were Vere & that our Cook knows them & I suppose inform'd their Ser^{vts} of ye behaviour of our Jacobin Landlord, for this instant I receive the following Polite Note, ' Mr Vere ye Banker finding himself so near Lady Newdigate takes ye liberty of making his respects to her L^{dp} to enquire after her health & to tender her any services in his Power.'

It is really a great Comfort, he will know exactly

what is right to do & will obviate all kinds of difficulties, for tho' I sh'd not like to give my own notes here, which might be disputed, he w^d ans^r them, so in Case we sh'd be obliged to Quit Brighton on Saturday & by any accident y^r further supply sh'd not arrive I can be in no distress. . . .

Mrs Mid.'s Rich^d, my Rich^d & Barret are separately walking ye town over, for as dear Milly had set her heart upon another Week we will stay if we can find a place to put our heads in, but I much doubt our success. To-morrow must decide it. . . . Miss Gros^r says ' Steyne is German for Stone.' She has seen in Old Maps ye Place spelt Brighthelmstein.

½ p^st 2 o'Clock. We have had a Blowing drive but not very unpleasant & have had a feast of Gooseberries & Bread, but no tidings yet of a house. Mid's Rich^d is in such a rage with ye Jacobin that I find he has been to a Lawyer of his acquaintance to ask whether I c^d be turn'd out. He call'd in Tryumph to tell me I c^d not. I knew it before but had rather do any thing than be subject to ye Man's impertinence, besides I shall inconvenience a family who are very innocent of all this. We are all very well but in a grand fuss you will suppose. . . . Huzza, Gregory for ever! The Civil Bookseller that I told you I subscribed to by mistake & who had lent me a Telescope has help'd me out of all our difficulties. He has taken a house for a family in London & was to write to-night to say when they may come. Hearing of our distress he has offer'd it me for a Week! It is lower down upon ye same Cliff, not so near ye Edge, nor so much exposed to ye wind. So ends our troubles. In consiquence of

Mr Vere's note we have offer'd ourselves to drink Tea with M^rs and Miss Veres this afternoon & are accepted.

Friday ye 4th.—We are preparing to get out of ye Jacobin's Clutches as soon as our Eyes open to-morrow morning. The People are not yet gone from ye house we are to occupy, so we have taken a pig in a poke, but it appears like this we are in, & we had Hopson's Choice. Y^e situation too is desirable, not 50 y^ds to move our things & ye Wind is again Calm so that our Sea View is enchanting. . . . We are all in love with old Vere. He w^d hand me into my own house, wch indeed I c^d hardly have enter'd without his help, ye Wind was so boisterous. Our Visit seem'd to please very much. . . .

The Acc^t from Wandon to-day is very uncomfortable. Y^e Crisis of ye fever may be on ye 14th day or go on to ye 21st & that Period is dreaded for ye Child whose death may occasion immediate Labor, & how y^e Mother's strength may bear it so weaken'd by y^e fever is very doubtful. Nelly guards her expressions as much as possible, but it is evident that Fanny is very bad & Nelly in very great anxiety of Mind. . . .

We far outdo Taylor's acc^t of y^e Hail Stones. Many here declare they measured $2\frac{1}{2}$ & 3 inches & Mr Vere says he measured one at Chichester that had lain many hours in his Room $1\frac{3}{4}$ inch & that £1,000 damage was done at Goodwood & Stansted. . . .

Sunday morning 6th.—You shall have y^e 1st fruits of my Pen from my New Lodgings which we were happily settled in last night. They are really pleasanter than those we have quitted ; je ne sais pas pourquoi, for it has exactly y^e same View but being lower on ye Cliff we feel ourselves more in ye Sea. What Dolphins! you will say. . . . It is certain I c^d not have been turn'd out, but the Man is a Jacobin whose principles are to restrain others but to obey no Laws but his own. He c^d not have turn'd me out but might have plagued me which he did to the last & now accuses me of stealing 24 Backgammon men, but we are out of his Clutches thank God & by means of our good friend Fairy both ourselves & serv^ts are Comfortably Lodged, for we c^d not decently contrive to put 3 men & 3 maids into 3 Beds. Fairy luckily has a Spare Bed & ye distance is so small that it is no inconvenience to us & I hope none to her as we are Early people. . . .

I am sorry poor Nelly's anxiety & attentions to the sick & to ye several numerous Branches of both families that she has to send Acc^ts to, sh'd make her so remiss to you. You seem in the Letter I have to-day to be still ignorant that Fanny's disorder is ye same fever that Lord Charles had & that her situation has made it from ye 1st a most hazzardous affair. The Death of the Child has been hourly expected; that event Kerr says w^d bring on immediately Labour, & seem'd to insinuate that it was ye most desirable, as ye Labour w^d probably be more Easy & short & they dread her strength being so much exhausted by ye fever as not to get safely through it. Nelly's words to-day are these 'Kerr's unexpected arrival at a Critical Moment last night seems to have been quite providential. The Apothecary saw a turn in Fanny's disorder which he thought required an immediate Change of Medecine. A messenger was despatch'd post to Northampton but before ye Man c^d reach Newport ye Doct^r arrived. Our Joy can be more easily conceived than described. Y*e* Apoth. was right, but Kerr quiets our apprehensions by assurances that symtoms are still favorable. He returns to us to-morrow & will sleep here. He does not pronounce possitively that this is ye Crisis; it may be so or may be protracted a few days Longer.' Surely this is a most Allarming Acc^t & Nelly's task a most Anxious and Laborious one. Thank God she continues well if we may believe her own acc^t which we resolve to do. Sh^d Poor Dear Fanny get over this fever, which indeed I much doubt & you are so good as to give us this full Latitude, I think we shall certainly go by Wandon & Drop Milly there, but not take Nelly B. into an infected house. Therefore I shall probably sleep at Woburn & either see Nelly there or go with Milly just to get a peep at her. Old People are not subject to Catch disorders, therefore I have no apprehension for myself or even for Milly, who must be about Lady Charles to be of real use, but if you have any scruples about me I will promise you not to see her; but it will be a relief to my mind to see Nelly & to hers also. Therefore I am sure you will wish me to do it. . . .

. *Monday 7th August.*—No Letters to-day so have little to write about. . . . Old Vere, his Wife 2 Nieces & a friend that is with them drank Tea with us yesterday. They are so fond of us they torment us to death with messages & invitations to drive out in their sociable, ride with ye young Ladies, walk with them upon ye Steyne etc. But they are in a stile far above us, come home at 5 o'Clock to Dinner & are out till 11 at night walking ye Steyne or Raffling for Bijoux at ye Booksellers, which is much y[e] fashion here. We carry poor Nell to none of these things, for when we do walk down to y[e] Steyne we leave it before the Great World arrive; but we had a ½ intention to take her to y[e] Ball to-night, as we hear it is to be a good one. Our Spirits are hardly up to it for in truth we are in a sad fright about Fanny. Pray God that to-morrow may bring better acc[ts]. . . .

Tuesday 8th.—I was dress'd for y[e] Ball, but a Nasty head ach (y[e] 1st I have had since I came here) seized me very suddenly, so as soon as I sent my Companions off I went to Bed, Slept it off & am well to-day. I know not what c[d] have caused it unless it was y[e] high & Cold Wind upon y[e] Downs or that I had worry'd myself about Wandon, which is not less y[e] case to-day. I wrote you our last Allarming, I think, acc[t]. Nelly said she w[d] write again on Sunday, w[ch] if she had done we sh'd have had it to-day. Her last was written on Thursday, Kerr was to be there on Friday & was to Sleep there & I find by a Letter I receive to-day from my Brother that y[e] Doct[r] expected friday to be a decisive day. If there had been any happy turn Nelly w[d] not have omitted giving us a Line on Sunday. I cannot help having fears also for dear Nelly. Let things turn out as they will we shall certainly leave this place on Saturday, but whether we shall visit Wootton our Wandon news will determine. A Letter will certainly find me in Town on Monday. Oh! the Vile Post Man! he has just brought y[e] enclosed which he had overlook'd. The Event I fear is but too Certain. I don't suppose we can do any good by making Woburn our Road. If not shall probably do as we first intended, stay 2 nights with Jessy & then make y[e] best of our way to Arbury. We are all three well but hurry'd as you will suppose & I must write a Line to my Poor Brother who is almost heart broken. He seems to have had Little or no hope for some time. . . .

Wednesday 9th August.—Reviving News from Wandon. Indeed I gave all up yesterday and so I think w^d you. Nelly's Words to-day are 'When Doct^r Kerr arrived yesterday (Sunday) he found ye pulse abated & some other favorable symtoms, & at 6 o'Clock this morning he came to my Bed Side to tell me that every good Sign was continu'd & that we had now everything to hope. The sudden transition from having everything to fear, has quite intoxicated both L^d Ch^s & me. We have taken Fanny up in a Blanket this Morn^g & Changed her Bedding. She has borne ye fatigue without any apparent Injury, says she feels herself in Heaven, & I hope will get some Sleep, a Blessing she has been very long a Stranger to.' There is good Ground for hope in this Acc^t most certainly, but yet we cannot compose our spirits enough to determine on a Visit to ye Evelyns. . . .

Mr Vere paid me a Visit this morn^g & beg'd I w^d not scruple drawing upon him for any Money I might want. I told him he was a bold man knowing so well ye various Ways of spending Money at this place. He answer'd that was ye very reason that led him to suspect that expenses might exceed my Calculations & that he w^d with pleasure answer my drafts to any amount. There's for you now. No bounds are to be set to my extravagance. . . .

Thursday 10th August.—. . . You begin to be Jealous & won't furnish me with a pretence to apply *to my friend,*

P

but I must tell you it is now too late to put a stop to ye intimacy, things have gone too far ; he has sent me to-day a Pine Apple, a Bunch of Grapes & 6 Apricots & I have ask'd Fairy & Miss Grosvenor to eat them. To-morrow being our last day we shall dine with ye former & leave our people to Pack. . . .

I sh'd have named Wandon first if we had heard to-day. I did not expect it, but shall certainly have news to report to-morrow. Pray God that it may be good. . . . God preserve you in health & happiness till I come to plague vou.

Lady Newdigate's letters from Brighton end cheerfully, but the hopes of Lady Charles's recovery were doomed to be overthrown in the next letter from Wandon. Indeed, she had already passed away on Wednesday, the day when Lady Newdigate was rejoicing in Nelly Mundy's hopeful account of the apparent rally on the previous Monday.

Fanny Mundy became Lady Charles FitzRoy in June 1795, and after two short years of married life she died on the 9th of August, 1797, leaving one son, born in 1796.

Lady Charles FitzRoy.

CHAPTER XV

1797—1800

Rich brown locks, passionate love, and deep early sorrow, strangely different as they seem from the scanty white hairs, the apathetic content, and the unexpectant acquiescence of old age, are but part of the same life's journey.—MR. GILFIL'S LOVE-STORY.

THE previous chapter contains the last cheery letters from Lady Newdigate to her husband whilst she continued in tolerable health. For the next three years she seems to have been constantly ailing and a source of anxiety to all who loved her. From her own showing in previous illnesses we may divine with what fortitude her brave spirit bore up against the trials of continuous physical discomfort. There is also ample evidence in the correspondence of contemporaries of her patience and cheerfulness under suffering.

Each year she seems to have tried the beneficial effect of some English watering-place, and we hear of her at Bath on more than one occasion; but as Sir Roger accompanied her to this fashionable resort for gouty and rheumatic patients, there are no letters chronicling her daily experience, as was her invariable habit.

In the summer of 1800 she made one more trial of the sea-bathing in which she had so much faith. This time the favoured spot was Margate, to which place she was conveyed from London by sailing packet. As usual, she made some stay at her brother's house in town, and was accompanied to Margate by her faithful sister Nelly Mundy. The younger Nelly, Milly Barton's daughter, had married her cousin, young Ned Mundy, in the March of this year, and they also seem to have been of the party to Margate.

At this time Lady Newdigate was often in acute suffering from dropsical complications, yet she seems to have written brightly and courageously as before to Sir Roger, who, now in his eighty-second year, remained at home. The only records he has preserved of this last batch of letters are a collection of extracts cut out of them, all bearing testimony to her love and gratitude towards himself, and her affection for her home at Arbury. These slips of paper are enclosed in a cover on which Sir Roger has written in the trembling hand of old age :

1800

Dulces exuviæ dum vita Deique sinebant
Voluntas Suprema.[1]

We here give one or two of the extracts from the mutilated letters :

You are a Dear Angel, I can read your thoughts in every line. It is all I wish & makes me doubly anxious to be enabled by a tollerable degree of returning health to reward you in some measure for all you have done & suffer'd for me. Did I not still entertain a Gleam of Hope that God in his great Mercy w^d in his good time extend his Goodness so far I sh'd most earnestly pray him to take me to himself that I might no longer be a Bar to your happiness & that of all who Love me. But he has with numberless other Blessings given me a never failling hope & Confidence that I shall yet enjoy some years of Ease & of happiness with you at dear Arbury, & with this hope I ought with patience to endure ye Tryal however long it may be.

Another cutting is evidently from the last letter she wrote before leaving Margate. The date of the post-mark on the back is 30th July, 1800.

Shall certainly send Luggage & those who wish to

---

[1] 'Sweet spoils whilst life and the supreme will of God permitted.'

Brave ye ocean by ye Packet & come away with those who are as Cowardly as myself in Hack Chaises. You are answerable for my Want of Courage. I used to have enough, but you make Life so very valuable to me that I cannot consent to hazzard it or neglect any means to preserve it, that depends on myself. God's Goodness to me has been so wonderfully great that I doubt not he will direct me for ye best & at all Events I hope we shall have a happy meeting on Saturday. We are going to dine with ye Mundys & Leave our People to pack & get all things on Board. . . . Our Cap^{tn} has just been here, he laughs at my apprehensions of a storm, says this is a fine Steady wind that will take us to London in about 12 or 14 hours . . . & now my Dear Soul do you & ye good & kind Jessy joyn your Prayers that I may have no more delays, but that we may have a happy meeting on Friday next. What joy there is in ye thought, Adieu.

The 'Gleam of Hope' Lady Newdigate still entertained for her ultimate return to health was not realised. She returned to Arbury and lived through the summer, but on the 30th of September the end came and she was released from a life of suffering.

By her Will (an informal document), dated 10th of March this same year (1800), she leaves various bequests to her family and friends, including 'the little syren.' She begins as follows:

I Hester Newdigate, Wife of Sr Roger Newdigate of Arbury in the County of Warwick B^t having my dear Husband's permission to dispose of the property he has generously given me, I do bequeath it in the following manner. . . .

Then follow the gifts of annuities of 50l. a year to

each of her sisters, Mrs. Oliver and Mrs. Barton, with various legacies from 20*l*. to 100*l*. to her Mundy nephews, and '£500 to my affectionate Eleve and Friend Sarah Shilton' with 'my small pianoforte & one of my Clavicellos.' She leaves several small legacies and gifts of jewellery, &c., to different friends, whilst the residue of her money and valuables was to go to her sister, Nelly Mundy. In this way she disposed of some 4,000*l*. worth of property.

On October 31, a month after her death, Nelly Mundy writes the following letter to Sir Roger:

MY DEAR SIR ROGER,—Tho' the motive of sending you the enclosed is good & *obvious*, I know not whether I can be justified in doing so. It is the Copy of a manuscript found in the Dear departed Angel's pocket book, written in her own hand & worn with use so as to be illegible in some places as the Copy shows. It has cost me many tears in transcribing, yet I think my Dear Sr Roger it must give you more pleasure than pain. If I have judged amiss in what I have done pray forgive the unintentional error of

Y^r very affectionate
& faithful
N. MUNDY.

Shipley.

Enclosed was the following paper:

Copy of Manuscript found in my Dear Sister's Pocket Book—much worn

Morning Prayer •

O Father of Mercies & God of all Comfort, the sweet refreshment of our Souls & constant support of our bodies—by thy goodness it is that I have been preserved the night past from all perils & dangers & that my frail body has been refresh'd with rest & lives to praise thee in another day. Great & boundless have been Thy mercies to me most gracious God. By thee I have been holden up ever since I was born, restrain'd & protected from innumerable evils into which the propensities of my corrupt nature might have led me. Placed at my birth & to this hour in situations of ease & comfort; blessed with the tenderest of Parents & the best & most affectionate of Husbands & kindest of friends, & throughout Life with a degree of happiness & prosperity so far surpassing the common lot of mortals & my own deserts, that my heart overflows with Gratitude unutterable. But above all I praise Thy Holy Name for the light of thy Glorious Gospel, & for the hope it has given me of obtaining Eternal Life through the merits of thy Son Jesus Christ. In an humble sense of my own unworthyness I desire with the profoundest reverence to acknowledge that thou, even in thy severest dispensations hast kind intentions & gracious designs towards us. It has pleased thee in Thy infinite Wisdom to lay thy afflicting hand upon me. Behold I fly unto thee for succour, accept with patient resignation this thy Visitation & most earnestly beseech thee to enable me to bear it with such submission as becomes a Creature & a Sinner & to sanctify all my afflictions to me, that this sickness of my body may be an increase of health to my Soul. To that end O Lord make me diligent in searching my heart that I may discover anything that is hateful in thy sight & on my true & sincere repentance I pray thee to remove thine anger from me, heal my Soul that has sinned against thee, & if it be not thy blessed will to heal my body also

& to restore peace & joy to my Dwelling, give me such perfect resignation as shall induce Thee in thy Mercy to mitigate the pains & sufferings of my declining state & when the time that thou hast appointed for my great Change shall come, do thou O Merciful God, Saviour strengthen [illegible] . . . support my Spirits & Confirm my faith in my Dying Agonies & through the merits of him who Dyed for me receive me into the Company of thy blessed saints & angels, into thy Heavenly Kingdom thro' Jesus Christ.

Shower down thy heavenly Benediction upon my most Dearly beloved Husband & if in thy Wisdom thou thinkest fit to deprive him of me, in whom, next to Thee, he looks for Support & Solace of his Old Age, do thou Gracious Lord grant him so great a supply of thy heavenly Comfort & consolation accompany'd with his good health, Chearful disposition & all other blessings that can make Life desirable to him, that the remainder of his days may pass as those already spent in that even peaceful tenor which only good men can experience.

I also implore thy Especial Blessing, Spiritual & temporal upon my dear Bro[r] Sisters & all my friends & relations: Sooth the afflictions of all those who will grieve for me & grant in mercy to them and to thy Unworthy Suppliant, that as long as thou seest fit to spare my Life, thou will vouchsafe such a degree of Ease & Comfort [unto me] that my declining state may be gentle & imperceptible & that I may be capable to the last of enjoying the Society of my Dearest friends & of being some Comfort to them. And grant that we may all so finish our Course here, that we may by thee be permitted to meet & know each other in a better world.

On the cover which enfolds this prayer, Sir Roger has written the date of his receiving it and the following Latin inscription :

1800 Novr 4th Rec^d

Semper honos nomenq [i.e. nomenque] tuum pietasq [pietasque] manebit ! [1]

Hester Newdigate is buried in Harefield Church, where she lies in the chancel, and the monument erected to her memory is a white alabaster urn designed by her husband. It is on a similar scale to that of Sir Roger's first wife, Sophia Conyers, and in the centre between the two is yet another, to the memory of his mother, Elizabeth (Twisden) Lady Newdigate.

Other memorials of Hester Newdigate still exist at Arbury. The fruits of her spinning-wheel may be seen in fine white table linen woven into damask cloth the year she died, and embroidered in one corner with the legend, 'Spun by Lady N. 1800.'

And every spring, in Nature's glorious resurrection-time, for more than a century past there has come up through the grass of Swanland—her special portion of the grounds at Arbury—a large H. N. outlined in golden daffodils, which tradition says were planted by herself.

[1] 'Ever shall thy honour and name and piety remain !'

CHAPTER XVI

1797–1806

'Ah! you remember well the Sunday as Mrs. Gilfil first come to church, eh Mrs. Patten?' 'To be sure I do. . . . I think I see him [Mr. Gilfil] now a-leadin' her up th' aisle an' her head not reachin' much above his elber: a little pale woman wi' eyes as black as sloes, an' yet lookin' blank-like as if she see'd nothin' wi' em.' 'I warrant she had her weddin' clothes on?' said Mr. Hackit. 'Nothin' pertickler smart—on'y a white hat tied down under her chin and a white Indy muslin gown. . . .

'Mr. Gilfil brought her to tea wi' me one afternoon and he says in his jovial way, " Now Mrs. Patten, I want Mrs. Gilfil to see the neatest house and drink the best cup o' tea in all Shepperton; you must show her your dairy and your cheese-room and then she shall sing you a song!" An' so she did; an' her voice seemed sometimes to fill the room an' then it went low an' soft, as if it was whisperin' close to your heart like.'

Mr. Gilfil's Love-story.

WE must turn back a year or two to take up the thread of 'the little syren's' life from the time she returned from Lisbon. The change of air and scene had been of great benefit to her health and spirits, but she still remained of too fragile an organisation to encourage any hopes on the part of her kind patrons that she would ever be able to undertake the perils and trials of a professional life. Her experimental visit to London when only seventeen seems to have been the first and last she made with this object in view.

Henceforward Sally's home was at Arbury, where we hear of her constantly as one of the family. Relations and friends of Sir Roger's and of Lady Newdigate's almost always include 'love to Sally' in their messages of remembrance in their letters. Mr. and Mrs. Francis Newdigate, writing from Italy in 1795-96, constantly refer to Sally's talent and taste when hearing new music.

'Tell Sally,' writes Mr. Newdigate, 'I am bringing her some roaring recitatives for the Hall at Arbury.' Thus, though never a professional singer, Sally seems to have had a considerable reputation in the county and neighbourhood as a gifted musician of no mean order.

In 1797 she went to assist at a musical party at Packington, the seat of the Earl of Aylesford.[1] On her return to Arbury she was the bearer of the following letter from her host:

DEAR SIR ROGER,—I must avail myself of Miss Shilton's good humor by desiring her to give this note to you for the purpose of assuring you that L^{dy} Aylesford and myself are exceedingly thankful to you & L^{dy} Newdigate for the very great entertainment we have had in your kind indulgence in allowing Miss Shilton to be of our musical party this week, to which we very justly ascribe the *great éclat* its performances have made. I hope you will find that Miss Shilton has not suffered in health by singing too much. It was the only thing to be apprehended from the pleasure it gave us and her good humor'd readiness, and I can really say that there was but one opinion of her singing and playing, tho' all the performers very justly complain that we were not applauded one half so much as we deserved.

L^{dy} Aylesford desires me add her best thanks to you and L^{dy} Newdigate

I am Dear Sir Roger
Yours very sincerely
AYLESFORD.

Sally was doubtless a great comfort to both Sir Roger and Lady Newdigate in the latter's prolonged illness, and probably she could not well be spared from her Arbury home until all cause for attendance on the invalid

[1] Heneage, fourth Earl of Aylesford.

had ended so sadly. Between three and four months after Lady Newdigate's death the event took place which forms the romantic climax to 'Mr. Gilfil's Love-story.' It was in January 1801 that Sally Shilton became the wife of Mr. Ebdell, the Vicar of Chilvers Coton (Shepperton in the tale), and went to live at the quaint old vicarage close to the church, which was only some three miles from her old home at Arbury.

A day or two after the marriage, we find letters written by both bride and bridegroom to Sir Roger expressing their mutual happiness. Sally writes with many dashes and some doubtful spelling:

I am sure my dear & Best of Benefactors will (I flatter myself) have no objection to my addressing him, to Convince him that I really feel the *Happiest of Beings* and I cannot help hoping & feeling *sure* that I *shall* ever be one. Mr. Ebdell is gone to a meeting at the Colledge [1] this morning; he I am delighted to tell you seems most *Compleatly happy*, and I shall ever make it my Constant study & wish for a Continuance. Indeed the Pangs I felt when you departed from me on Monday were great; and I could not summons up sufficient Resolution to accompany you to y^r Carriage. I hope you were not angry with me, for my Little Heart was too, *too* full I assure you.

My *Dear Husband*, but what a strange word! is very kind & Indulgent to me and I hope I shall ever prove grateful for his very kind attention to me.

I cannot sufficiently express the Gratitude I feel for all your Fatherly Goodness & kindness I have for so many years experienced; and be assured I shall ever make it my Constant Prayer to merit all the Blessings bestowed upon me.

---

[1] ' The workhouse, euphuistically called the " College." '—*G. Eliot.* Now still called ' College for the Poor.'

The weather being so indifferent we are determined not to go to Birmingham. I think with y^r Permission I might come to Arbury to-morrow morning after Breakfast and Mr Ebdell will I am sure accompany me.

I have been very Busy settling myself in *my own House* which indeed is Vastly Comfortable. Will you have the Goodness to send my Piano Forte for Mr Ebdell wishes it was here very often. I beg you will accept of our Best Thanks for the very acceptable and agreeable Present you were so kind to send; the Venison is excellent.

Well, God bless you my Dear Sir
           & Believe me to be
               Y^r ever Grateful affc^{te} *Daughter*
                              S. EBDELL.

Chilvers Coton
    Wensday morning.

Mr. Ebdell writes at the same time:

SIR,—Altho' Sally is in her own Room writing I believe to her Friends at Arbury I cannot resist the violent inclination I feel to thank you most sincerely for the very valuable present you have made to me in her, under my own hand. And to inform you that She really is comfortable & happy. It is true she sometimes heaves a sigh for the Friends she has left, which to me is rather pleasing than otherwise, as indicating the natural goodness of her grateful Heart. It wou'd be strange indeed if I cou'd not with truth in this early stage, profess my compleat satisfaction & Happiness, but as there surely are probable reasons to expect a continuance of our mutual

Felicity—that you may live long in Health to hear these same professions shall be the constant & most earnest Prayer of

    Your most obliged & grateful
      Humble Servant B. G. EBDELL.

After the death of Lady Newdigate and the marriage of Sally, Sir Roger's life would naturally have been a lonely one. Being the youngest of his family and at this time in his eighty-second year, his three elder sisters had long predeceased him. Moreover, owing to causes difficult to explain, Sir Roger had not been on the best of terms with his nearest relations for a long time past. The few remaining years of his life would have been solitary indeed had it not been for the friendship and companionship of his cousin Francis Newdigate, of Kirk Hallam, with that of his wife and only son. At his request they came to live with him at Arbury, and at Sir Roger's death Francis Newdigate succeeded to the Warwickshire property, but for his lifetime only.[1]

In July 1805 the county and neighbourhood were much excited by the prospect of a visit to Warwickshire by King George III.

Lord Aylesford was to have the honour of receiving the King at Packington, and wrote to tell Sir Roger of the arrangements to be made for the occasion.

          Packington, 30th June.

DEAR SIR ROGER NEWDIGATE,—I daresay you know our Good King proposes to honor this County with a Visit, but perhaps you have not heard the plan he at present has lined unless something unforseen makes it necessary to change it. He is to be at Warwick on the Tuesday after he leaves London and on the Wednesday to receive the address of the Corporation of Coventry in St. Mary's

---

[1] The property being entailed on Charles Parker's descendants passed to his grandson, Charles Newdigate Newdegate, on the death of Francis Newdigate in 1835.

Hall, and from thence to proceed to my House—from thence to Lichfield and Birmingham.

If the Parliament's sitting will allow it He will be at my house on the 17th: if not a week later.

It does not appear to me that you can any way pay your devoirs to the King more conveniently to yourself than while he is at Packington and therefore beg to propose to you to dine that day at my house at the L^d of the Bedchamber's table. You will have an opportunity of making your bow early in the afternoon so as to incur no risque in your return home. I wish I could offer you a bed but considering how large a family I have at home and how large a company I am to be housed with, I do not feel my vanity mortified in confessing I have not a bed to spare. But allow me to assure you that if what I have proposed meets your approbation, it will give me great pleasure.

I am etc. etc.

AYLESFORD.

Sir Roger evidently thought the occasion of this correspondence too important not to preserve a copy of his answer, which runs as follows:

Arbury, 3rd July 1805.

DEAR L^D AYLESFORD,—I am at a loss to express my gratitude to your Lordship for your obliging invitation or my regret in being forced to decline that honor. If I had been able I should not have fail'd long ago to acknowledge your repeated goodness, by paying my respects to your Lordship at Packington. But I have not for a long time gone farther from home than my Parish Church & grow weaker every day, & in my 87th year I am neither fit nor able to join the splendid Court at Packington. But no one can be more truly thankful for the honor of his Majesty's visit to the County, or join more sincerely in prayers & heartfelt wishes for a long continuance of his Health & Reign over us.

With your Lordship's permission Mr. Newdigate will wait upon you at Packington in the afternoon of the 17th to make my Apology to the King & offer of duty & service as a Magistrate & Major of Volunteers.

Sensible how great a burden will be laid upon you, I flatter myself you will not take it amiss the liberty I have taken of sending this by Barrs my Steward, with orders to make enquiries in your Lordship's Family whether anything that Arbury can furnish may be agreable or usefull upon this great occasion.

In my Stores I have a tolerable Crop of Peaches, Nectarines & Grapes & Pines. To send you Fish is to send Coals to Newcastle, but if perchance your Stews were deficient I have plenty of good Carp ready at all times. If my Butler or any of my Servts can be usefull you will Command them.

One thing more occurs to me, knowing how greatly Music is in favour, you will perhaps entertain your royal Guests with a Concert or private Airs, in which case give me leave to remind you that I have in my neighbourhood a most charming little Siren who would be highly honored by your Lordship's commands as will Mr. Ebdell her husband. If you approve and will fix your Hour, I will prevail upon her to take my Chaise to wait upon you, & bring her back again.

I will not take more of your time than to assure you that it will give me real pleasure if in any respects I can contribute to your Lordship's pleasure or convenience.

I am my Lord
Your affec^{ate} & much obliged
humble servant
R. NEWDIGATE.

In the end the King's proposed visit fell through, which was communicated to Sir Roger by Lord Aylesford in the next letter.

Packington, July 6, 1805.

DEAR SIR ROGER NEWDIGATE,—Your letter which was brought by Mr. Barrs has imposed upon me the most difficult task for I know not how to express all that I feel on receiving so much friendship and kindness, or how to thank you for so obliging and profuse an offer. I delayed writing till to-day, because I had the same day that Mr Barrs was here received a letter intimating some doubts whether His Majesty could prudently undertake this excursion. To-day I have received a letter from Ld Hawkesbury to acquaint me that He had received His Majesty's commands to inform me that in consequence of the Complaint in his Eyes He has judged it most prudent to defer his journey till another Year. He is going immediately to Weymouth. I have by the same post received a letter from a Person who has very good information, which I hope in God will prove so in this instance, in which he tells me 'since writing the above I have heard with infinite satisfaction that Mr. Phipps has declared H. M.'s eyes to be in no danger, & that he will soon have perfect sight.'

I must confess the disappointment at not having the honor of seeing him under my roof I feel very much, but I love and value him too much to let any private wishes of my own suffer me to repine at what evidently is the wisest and most prudent step he can take to avoid heat and fatigue—and tho' under this alteration I cannot avail myself of any part of your friendly & generous offer I shall always remember it with pleasure & gratitude.

   I am dear Sir Roger
    Your most obliged & faithful servant
      AYLESFORD.

We now approach the last scene of Sir Roger's long life. A year later, in July 1806, he writes of himself to a friend:

I thank my good God my prayer is heard! I am unwell but have no particular complaint, but a general defailance, gradual decay, increasing weakness; but by His great mercy my road down hill is easy. I have only to look one way and to pray 'Lord let Thy servant depart in peace.' . . .

'When his last malady came upon him, which was attended, through God's mercy, with little bodily suffering, those who were near beheld him as aforetime, affectionate, pious, and resigned, "longing," as he expressed himself, "to have the curtain closed." And on Tuesday, November 25, about half past 11 at night, without a pang or struggle he breathed his last.'[1]

---

[1] From Archdeacon Churton's 'Memoirs of Sir R. Newdigate' in the *Gentleman's Magazine*, 1807.

CONCLUSION

IN the foregoing chapters our readers will have found the materials for a far more intimate and authentic knowledge of the lives and characters of the real Cheverels of Cheverel Manor than ever had George Eliot.

It may be interesting to trace briefly where the authoress remained true to facts in regard to the principal actors in her tale, and where she diverged into the realms of her own imagination.

To begin with the heroine of ' Mr. Gilfil's Love-story ' :

CATERINA

The little syren's gift of song, her adoption as a child by Sir Roger and Lady Newdigate on account of her beautiful voice, and her ultimate marriage to the vicar of the parish are well-known facts. All we learn from Lady Newdigate's letters and Sally's own artless productions tend to confirm our impressions of Caterina in the story as a highly gifted and personally attractive young songstress, though fragile in form and of a delicate constitution. It seems more than probable that so sensitive and impressionable a nature as was Sally's may have undergone some acute love-disappointment, though possibly undiscovered by Lady Newdigate. Her simple charms and undeniably beautiful voice were very likely to have attracted the thoughtless attentions of some gay Adonis, who, whilst amusing himself with a passing flirtation, may have kindled feelings both real and deep in the girl's tender heart.

Sally's lengthened stay at Lisbon when eighteen years old may have been undertaken as much for the cure of a wounded heart by change of scene as for her restoration to health by removal to a more balmy air. The experiment seems to have succeeded in its object, but it was not until eight years later that Sally rewarded the devotion of Sir Roger's chaplain and the vicar of his parish by becoming Mrs. Ebdell.

In the pretty letter from the newly married wife to Sir Roger it may be thought she seems over anxious to impress upon her old friend that she is really happy, almost leading one to suspect this is a case in which 'the lady protests too much.' Still we have no reason to believe the marriage was anything but a success during her twenty-two years of married life, for we are obliged to admit that Mrs. Ebdell did not die in the flower of her youth, but at the less romantic age of forty-nine. During the many years she lived as mistress of the old vicarage she had time to imprint her story, her attractive looks, and her fine voice on the minds of the parishioners, of which faint memories have been handed down to the present day.

Bernard Gilpin Ebdell and Sarah his wife are buried in their parish church, and a monument to their memory is placed above what used to be the vicarage pew. They had one child, a daughter, Anne, born in 1807. She, too, has left a picturesque impression behind her. The children of her contemporaries still bear in mind the description given them of this young girl as she usually appeared at church, in a white spun silk shawl with a red rose at her breast. Anne Ebdell married Mr. Latimer Harpur, the brother of George Eliot's 'secondary squire of the parish,' and some of Mr. Ebdell's descendants still occasionally revisit the scene of their grandfather's love-story.

Captain Wybrow

There are many points of resemblance between Captain Wybrow in the story and the real Charles Parker. Amongst them may be quoted similarity in appearance from personal description; a like destiny in being selected as heir to the childless baronet; and a premature and unexpected death. But here the parallel ceases. We cannot find any ground for believing that Charles Parker ever trifled with the affections of the little syren. Indeed she was but eleven years old when he married Miss Anstruther, in 1785, and consequently if there was any foundation for the supposition that Sally's health suffered from a love-disappointment the author of it was not very likely to have been Charles Parker.

Lady Cheverel

If George Eliot's representation of Lady Cheverel is intended to be an accurate reproduction of Hester Lady Newdigate, we may justly think it is an unappreciative portrait and even less than kind.

Hester's frank outpourings in her letters reveal a warmer hearted and more affectionate disposition than we should have divined from our authoress's description of the stately lady with the 'expression of hauteur' uncontradicted by 'the cold grey eye.' Probably Hester's many illnesses and a natural dignity of manner and deportment may have prevented her character being rightly read and duly appreciated by her subordinates. We have also to bear in mind that George Eliot's impressions must have been derived from household gossip carried down to the next generation. Therefore we cannot wonder at a certain amount of ignorance and misconception in regard to the Lady of Cheverel Manor. On many points the story and the letters are completely in accord, such as in the prominence given to Lady Cheverel's remarkable musical taste and knowledge; her adoption of a little girl on account of her beautiful voice; the tact with which she manages her husband's crotchets; and the extreme deference she always shows to his wishes, great and small.

But we who have read her letters know the real Lady Newdigate to have been a truly affectionate wife, a loving and beloved sister, and when suffering had subdued and chastened her buoyant spirit, still brave and cheerful to the end, yet entirely resigned to the Divine Will.

Sir Christopher Cheverel

Sir Roger Newdigate was a subject easy to depict from life. Being endowed by nature with a fine presence and a genial disposition, he had all the superficial elements for ensuring popularity amongst his inferiors. Added to these gifts his strong personality and originality of character could not fail to make their mark during the eighty-seven years he lived in the midst of his tenants and villagers.

George Eliot seems to have realised him thoroughly, though only from tradition, for her father did not come into Warwickshire until after Sir Roger's death. The truthfulness of her picture is evidenced by those graphic touches in which she shows us the man with all his failings as well as his sterling worth. We recognise his optimistic nature in Sir Christopher's mistaken estimate of Miss Assher's character:

'Accustomed to view people who entered into his plans by the pleasant light which his own strong will and bright hopefulness were casting on the future, he saw nothing but personal charms and promising domestic qualities in Miss Assher, whose quickness of eye and taste in externals formed a real ground of sympathy between her and Sir Christopher.'

In another passage, referring to the old baronet's choice of Captain Wybrow as his heir, he is described as 'moved to the step I am sorry to say by an implacable quarrel with his elder sister, for a power of forgiveness was not among Sir Christopher's virtues.'

But later, when Sir Christopher loses his nephew sadly and unexpectedly, George Eliot does full justice to his warm, generous nature under the crushing blow: 'I'm very weak, Maynard—God help me! I didn't think anything would unman me in this way, but I'd built everything on that lad.... Perhaps I've been wrong in not forgiving my sister. She lost one of *her* sons a little while ago. I've been too proud and obstinate.'

Taken altogether, the original of Sir Christopher Cheverel receives ample justice from the gifted authoress's pen, though it is not as a county magnate, or as a well-known classical scholar, nor as a benefactor to Oxford that she celebrates his renown. Probably those from whom she got her information cared not much for any of these things. It is chiefly as an honest, kindly, independent English squire that she represents him to us, strictly just in his firm but benignant rule on his estate, and generous withal in spite of his unbending will.

Nowhere does George Eliot depict his character in more telling words than when she is describing the chief hobby of Sir Roger's life—the alteration and adornment of his ancestral home.

'As for Sir Christopher,' she writes, 'he was perfectly indifferent to criticism. "An obstinate crotchety man," said the neighbours. But I, who have seen Cheverel Manor as he bequeathed it to his heirs, rather attribute that unswerving architectural purpose of his, conceived and carried out through long years of systematic personal exertion, to something of the fervour of genius as well as inflexibility of will; and in walking through these rooms, with their splendid ceilings and their meagre furniture which tell how all the spare money had been absorbed before personal comfort was thought of, I have felt that there dwelt in this old English baronet some of the sublime spirit which distinguishes art from luxury and worships beauty apart from self-indulgence.'

The annals of the Cheverels of Cheverel Manor have come to their natural end. We have followed their fortunes from birth to death, not without learning something, we trust, from their simple straightforward lives.

Fortunately for them and for us, they were blissfully unconscious of the publicity in store for them a century later, when their life-story would provide a theme for the genius of one of England's most gifted novelists. In the letters we have transcribed there is no self-consciousness, no posing for effect before a wider tribunal than that of the indulgent relatives for whom alone they were written. Faulty as the spelling and syntax often are, they lay bare the hearts and lives of God-fearing, honest, loyal English men and women.

If not unduly presumptuous, we would cherish a hope that these autobiographical letters, with their charm of individuality and truth, may possibly 'gladden and chasten hearts in years to come' though unidealised by the pen of a George Eliot.

www.ingramcontent.com/pod-product-compliance
Lightning Source LLC
Chambersburg PA
CBHW032222230426
43666CB00033B/699